ISLAMIC MEDICAL ETHICS IN THE TWENTIETH CENTURY

SOCIAL, ECONOMIC AND POLITICAL STUDIES OF THE MIDDLE EAST

ÉTUDES SOCIALES, ÉCONOMIQUES ET POLITIQUES DU MOYEN ORIENT

VOLUME XLVI

TUTA SUB AEGIDE PALLAS · 1683 ·

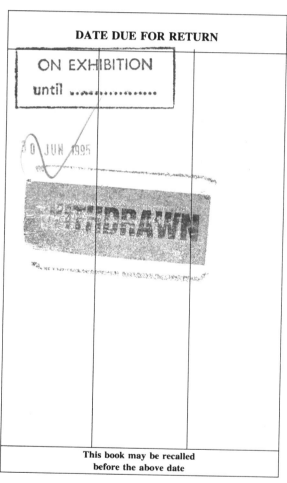

ISLAMIC MEDICAL ETHICS IN THE TWENTIETH CENTURY

BY

VARDIT RISPLER-CHAIM

E.J. BRILL
LEIDEN • NEW YORK • KÖLN
1993

The paper in this book meets the guidelines for permanence and durability of the Committee on Production Guidelines for Book Longevity of the Council on Library Resources.

Library of Congress Cataloging-in-Publication Data

Rispler-Chaim, Vardit.
Islamic Medical Ethics in the Twentieth Century / by Vardit Rispler-Chaim.
p. cm. — (Social, economic, and political studies of the Middle East. ISSN 0085-6193 ; v. 46 = Etudes sociales, économiques et politiques du Moyen Orient ; 46)
Includes bibliographical references and index.
ISBN 9004096086
1. Islamic ethics. 2. Medical ethics I. Title. II. Series: Social, economic, and political studies of the Middle East ; 46.
R725.59.R58 1993
174'.2'0917671—dc20 92-47108
CIP

Die Deutsche Bibliothek - CIP-Einheitsaufnahme

Rispler-Ḥayyîm, Wardīt:
Islamic medical ethics in the twentieth century / by Vardit Rispler-Chaim. — Leiden; New York; Köln: Brill, 1993
(Social, economic, and political studies of the Middle East; Vol. 46)
ISBN 90-04-09608-6
NR: GT

ISSN 0085-6193
ISBN 90 04 09608 6

PRINTED IN THE NETHERLANDS

CONTENTS

PREFACE

While I alone am responsible for the contents of this book on contemporary Islamic medical ethics and the ideas it expresses, it would not have been completed without the assistance of the following people and institutions, to whom I feel deeply indebted and wish to thank.

I am grateful to the staff of the Moshe Dayan Center for Middle Eastern and African Studies at Tel Aviv University for permitting me to use their archives of Arabic periodicals and newspapers. Special thanks are due to Mr. Haim Gal, Director of the Archives, who was ever willing to share his outstanding knowledge of the publications of the Arab world.

I am also grateful to Mr. Murray Rosovsky and Mrs. Diane Shubinsky who so meticulously edited the English text.

The book could never have reached its final form without the punctual and patient typing of Mrs. Heather Kernoff and Mrs. Danielle Friedlander.

Thanks are also due to Prof. D. Kushner, Dean of Humanities at the University of Haifa, and Prof. S. Waterman, Chairman of the Jewish-Arab Center at the University of Haifa, for granting me the subsidy for the publication of the book.

I am grateful to Dr. Ibrahim Geries, Chairman of the Department of Arabic at the University of Haifa, to my colleagues in the Department, and the secretary, for believing in the project and allowing me the free time to accomplish it.

Finally, warmest thanks go to my brother, Dr. S. Rispler, M.D., who often explained the medical terminology to me, and to my husband Rachman Chaim, who encouraged me all along.

Vardit Rispler-Chaim
Haifa, 1992

CHAPTER ONE

INTRODUCTION

Medicine is an ancient field of human practice and scholarship which has always striven to improve or correct the functioning of the human body. The search for a better understanding of the body faculties is driven by the human instinct for survival. The science of medicine has since ancient times been constantly developing. Each generation tries to learn from its predecessor and also to contribute something new. The medicine of a given civilization is usually an adaptation of medical knowledge collected from previous civilizations with the addition of achievements and discoveries of its own. Therefore, it is reasonable to expect that medicine of various civilizations will possess common denominators. But experience shows that each civilization develops medicine that is slightly different from the others'. Differences are due to cultural, religious, biological, and even financial factors.

The medicine of medieval times, for example, was mainly a derivative of Greek medicine shaded with Catholic colors. (Greek medicine itself was the heritage of other ancient medicines, such as the Egyptian, the Babylonian and the Assyrian.) Hence, medieval Jewish and Islamic medicines have much in common, but they are by no means identical. Both their similarities and peculiarities are very obvious.

Nowadays this trend is even more apparent. Western medicine as taught in the US and Western Europe proliferates all over the world. But medicine in the US can still easily be distinguished from medicine in Asia or Africa, and even from medicine in parts of Europe itself.

Although it is true today that wealth can bring Western medicine into remote areas of Asia and Africa, when this occurs it affects only a very narrow elite. When we consider medicine we prefer to think of it as the usage of large societies. For most of the populations of Africa and Asia, for example, the Western medicine that is offered is quite limited.

But resources are not the only reason why one body of medicine varies from another. Medical doctrine grows in a particular society, which fosters unique religious, cultural and philosophical ideas, and these greatly influence medical teaching and practice. Medicine in Ireland may be different from that in England, though both are located in Western Europe. This means that the medical ethics, or the moral and spiritual principles which guide practitioners and patients in the two countries, differ—even though the doctors in both societies may have graduated from the same medical schools.

Despite claims that nowadays medicine is a secular field of scholarship,[1] so that it approximates societies and helps bridge their differences, we hear of Catholic hospitals,[2] which adhere to Catholic ethics as distinct from other Christian ethics, and of Jewish ethics,[3] which are based on Biblical and Talmudic elements. We also hear of Hindu and Buddhist medical ethics, and of African medical ethics, etc.[4]

In the Middle Ages several authors wrote on Islamic medical ethics. Among them are Al-Ruhawī, Al-Ṭabarī, Al-Majūsī, Ibn Riḍwān Al-Baghdādī and Ibn Abī Uṣaybiʿa.[5] There is little literature on contemporary Islamic medical ethics.[6]

I claim that since there is an Islamic medicine which is based on Greek medicine but also on Qurʾanic teachings and on the model set by the Prophet Muhammad in the Hadith[7]—a fact revalidated today at international conferences of Muslims on Islamic medicine, there must also be an Islamic medical ethics which responds to the questions which Islamic medicine faces.

Moreover, I accept the evolutionary attitude in ethics, as suggested by H.A. Shenkin, for example,[8] and conclude that contemporary Isla-

---

[1] Robert M. Veatch (ed.), *Medical Ethics*, Jones and Bartlett Publishers Inc., Boston 1989, p. 15; H. Tristram Engelhardt Jr., "The Emergence of Secular Bioethics", in: Tom L. Beauchamp and LeRoy Walters (eds.), *Contemporary Issues in Bioethics*, USA 1989, p. 65.

[2] Charles J. McFadden, *Medical Ethics*, 6th edition, USA 1967, pp. 439-446.

[3] Fred Rosner, *Modern Medicine and Jewish Law*, New York 1972; Immanuel Jakobovits, *Jewish medical Ethics*, New York 1975.

[4] Robert M. Veatch (ed.), *Medical Ethics*, pp. 17-19.

[5] Samuel P. Asper and Fuad Sami Haddad, "History of Medical Ethics: Contemporary Arab World", in: Warren T. Reich (ed.), *Encyclopaedia of Bioethics*, New York 1978, v. 2, pp. 888-891; Abdul Hamid, "Medical Ethics in Islam", in: *Studies in History and Medicine*, Tughlaqabad New Delhi Dept. of History and Medicine, June 1981, p. 153.

[6] Several treatises discuss aspects of sexuality in Islam, but consider them more as social issues than medical.

[7] The same idea is held, for example, by Munawar Ahmad Anees, "Islamic medicine—The Placebo Effect", in: *Afkar Inquiry* 1986, 3 (10), pp. 34-39.

[8] *Medical Ethics: Evolution, Rights and the Physician*, Kluwer Academic Publishers, The Netherlands 1991.

mic medical ethics is necessarily different from medieval ethics, and so deserves to be studied periodically.

This book contains the conclusions of the study of contemporary Islamic medical ethics. The dynamics of the ethics will be shown in each of the fields of investigation. In fact, the "conclusions" should not be taken as final. They apply only as far as my research has gone, because ethics constantly changes as it reacts to circumstances, which are seldom static.

One of the difficulties in tracing contemporary Islamic ethics is the understandable dearth of written material on the subject. I found, however, that contemporary legal responses (*fatāwā*) largely provide the necessary information on most Islamic medical ethics. The *fatwā* literature, a branch of Islamic law, deals with many topics, not only medical. For the study of twentieth century Islam it is almost the only channel through which Muslim scholars' attitudes and legal opinions can be learned.

The *fatwā* lexically is an explanation or a clarification of some issue. The way it is generated is that one person asks a question—*istiftā'*—and the one responsible for the answer, responds (the *muftī*). The act of answering is termed *iftā'* and the answer itself is the *fatwā*.[9]

The *muftī* must be legally mature, a Muslim, a reliable trustworthy person who never sinned, learned in Islamic law, is of sound mind and proper conduct, and capable of comprehending one thing from another and of drawing conclusions. When he always adheres to one school of law he is labeled *ghayr mustaqill* (not independent); while as when he makes decisions based on Shar'ī data only, not bound by others' views, he is considered an independent *muftī* (*mustaqill*).[10]

Most of the *muftī*s whom I quote in this book tried to ground their opinions in an existing Shar'ī statement which might bear a direct or an indirect relevance to the subject at stake. In other words, very few *muftī*s can be called "independent".[11]

Does this mean that the *muftī*s of our time are not courageous or bold enough to formulate opinions independently of the classical legal heritage? Or is it that the public awaiting *fatāwā* is more suspicious of

---

9 Ibn Ṣalāḥ Al-Shahrazūrī (d. 643H), *Adab Al-Muftī wal Mustaftī*, 1st edition, n.p. 1986, pp. 23-24.

10 Ibid., pp. 86-87.

11 This is apparently in agreement with Al-Suyūṭī, who claimed that the independent *mujtahid* did not exist any longer in his time (15th century!). Others claim that Al-Shāfi'ī himself (d. 820) was the last independent *mujtahid* (ibid., p. 91).

unreferenced ideas and consequently the *muftīs* are forced to provide some Sharʿī support for any of their views, even at the price of combining for this purpose remote issues?

Regardless of the answers to these questions, what it definitely means is that there is much debate on-going among the *muftīs* themselves on almost every subject. The Sharʿī reference is used as a tool in the hands of the *muftī* to challenge his opponents or to better prepare himself to refute counter claims.

One of the greatest advantages of the *fatwā* literature, as already mentioned, is that it assumes a dialogue between lay people and scholars (since the basic format of the *fatwā* requires that the former ask, or are reported to have asked, questions, to which the latter respond). The scholars therefore tend to be as explicit as possible and a topic may be discussed more than once, whenever demanded, and by various scholars in various methodological and literary styles. When the *mustaftī* hears the answer which the *muftī* provided, he is not obliged to act according to it. Only if the asker is convinced of the truth of the answer, is he bound by it. In other words, no *fatwā* is final. One can always consult another *muftī* on an issue, and even one *muftī* when asked twice about the same matter, might change his mind. However, it is likely that one will ask a *muftī* whom one trusts.[12] This multiplicity of opinions allows the researcher several angles to a subject and even a semi-historical survey of how the subject has been approached over a certain period.

Most of my sources are *fatāwā* gathered from Egyptian newspapers and periodicals. The Egyptian publications were selected because of the central role Egyptian scholars play in the spiritual life of the whole Islamic world. Non-Egyptian sources are mentioned when they enrich the discussion. The period which this research covers is the twentieth century, with special emphasis on the 1980s and 1990s.

The most accessible sources for *fatāwā* are the various collections of *fatāwā* which are either the *fatāwā* of one *muftī*—such are the collections of Riḍā, Maḥmūd Shaltūt, Al-Shaʿrāwī, Maʾmūn, and Al-Qirḍāwī—or *fatāwā* collections which cover a certain period and are compiled by a formal religious institution. The latter obviously include *fatāwā* by various *muftīs*. To this type belong the Egyptian series *Al-Fatāwā Al-Islāmiyya* on its numerous volumes, and *Fatāwā*

---

[12] Ibid., pp. 166-168.

Islāmiyya liMajmūʿa min Al-Ulamāʾ Al-Afāḍil (issued by Saudi scholars).

The only disadvantage of these collections is that they contain all the *fatāwā* issued during several given years, thus it is quite likely that we have already encountered them in other forms of publication beforehand. These collections, therefore, lack novelty.

More authentic are the *fatāwā* which appear in newspapers and periodicals. These are also hard to trace because when they are published they are often surrounded by abundant journalistic material and religious reports which are not necessarily *fatwā*s.

In certain newspapers and journals the *fatāwā* appear under fixed columns, a fact which facilitates tracing them. Such are the columns "fikr dīnī" and "ṣafḥat Ramaḍān" in *Al-Ahrām*, "Suʾāl wajawāb" in *Al-Jumhūriyya*, "Fatāwā" in *Al-Umma Al-Islāmiyya*, "Fatāwā waAḥkām" in *Māyū*, etc.

In other periodicals and papers there is no fixed pagination for *fatāwā*. Such are *Majallat Al-Tawḥīd, Al-Daʿwa, Al-Jumʿa, Al-Nūr, Liwāʾ Al-Islām*, etc.

Even those publications which print *fatāwā* do not always do it on a regular basis. Rather, *fatāwā* would be published in them a few times a week, sometimes on the same weekdays but not always so.

When *fatāwā* are after all located, despite this sporadic manner of publication, they may or may not refer to a medical issue. The majority of *fatāwā* is naturally *not* about medical problems, but rather about various issues which interest Muslims. Medical ethics is one among many such issues.

The "detective" nature of collecting sporadic *fatāwā* renders it likely that some *fatwā*s have been overlooked. In other words, we cannot claim that we succeeded in gathering all the *fatwā*s that have been published on medical ethics, even with the limitations on place and time as explained before. We hope to have found many of them, including the most important ones—those that were quoted and referred to by other *muftī*s and led to the production of new *fatwā*s, whether enforcing or debating the original.

In some publications, the *muftī*'s name is mentioned with the content of his *fatwā* (for example in *Al-Ahrām*, *Majallat Al-Azhar* and *Majallat Al-Tawḥīd*). In others the *muftī*'s name is never or seldom mentioned (see *Al-Taṣawwuf Al-Islāmī*, *Al-Nūr*, *Al-Umma Al-Islāmiyya*, to mention only a few). There are publications which demonstrate no consistency in publishing/omitting the *muftī*'s identify. (Such as *Al-Jum'a, Al-Liwā' Al-Islāmī*, etc.).

It is difficult to conclude whether these differences result from differences in literary style only, or whether they derive from more substantial political-religious motives.

Although it is easy to classify the *muftī*s and the respective publications in which their *fatwā*s appeared to those that are government-approved and those that are not, i.e. to "establishment" *muftī*s, or for the same purpose fundamentalist *muftī*s, although more typical are the debates between "establishment" *muftī*s versus fundamentalist ones—debates over one medical point may run between two or more *muftī*s who are "establishment" *muftī*s and "fundamentalists" ones.

The governments role in formulating medical ethics—if it exists—has been handed over to the *muftī*s, who are eager to participate in this public endeavor and thus maintain their influence in an otherwise secularizing society. The *muftī*s are therefore our main source of information on medical ethics, in consensus and disputes alike.

The chapters of the book are various aspects of medical ethics, and each chapter is dedicated to one aspect and its related derivatives.

The reader will realize that not all aspects of medical ethics are covered in this book. This is mainly owing to insufficient data at present in the Islamic sources about these "missing" elements. Topics such as medical experiments on animals or on human beings, genetic engineering, mental disorders and aging, to mention only a few, must await further research.

CHAPTER TWO

ABORTIONS

Owing to the drive to control birthrates and the awareness among contemporary Muslims of the relative clinical ease of performing abortions as a means of solving personal difficulties, it has often been asked if the Islamic law (Sharīʿa) permits abortion or not.

Since questions pertaining to the legitimacy/morality of abortions are presented to religious figures and not to the physicians who perform abortions, there is obviously no interest in the surgical procedure itself, nor in its impact upon the woman's health or her future pregnancies. The only concern is whether the Sharīʿa is supportive of the operation or not.

From this general question the following related sub-questions arise: How long is a pregnancy? At what stage along the pregnancy does the fetus become a human being, from the Islamic legal point of view? What are the circumstances in which Islamic law permits abortion, and in what circumstances is abortion prohibited? Does the physician who suggests, approves, or performs the abortion bear liability for participation in a homicide? Is sterilization recommended as a means of preserving the health of a woman whose life is otherwise threatened by repeated abortions? The answers to these questions will in fact wholly convey the stand of the Sharīʿa on abortions.

Abortion (*ijhāḍ* or *saqṭ)* is medically defined as the "ejection of the contents of pregnancy before the completion of 28 weeks since last menstrual period."[1] Sometimes the abortion is "natural" (i.e., a miscarriage); either the body rejects the fetus, or the fetus stops growing and then drops out, but external interference of neither the mother nor the doctor is indicated. Such an abortion is perceived as an expression of God's will. It is thus the fault of no one.

However, our concern here is only with premeditated abortions (by the mother or both parents), which a doctor performs utilizing violent means to terminate the life of the fetus while it is still in its mother's

---

[1] Dr. Muḥammad ʿAlī Al-Bār, *Khalq Al-Insān bayna Al-Ṭibb wal Qurʾān*, 2nd edition, Saudi Arabia 1981, p. 211.

womb. It is this type of abortion which evokes a fierce debate among Muslim jurists. The following are some of the issues which this debate entails.

The duration of pregnancy

In the Middle Ages most of the *fuqahā'* (jurists) believed that a pregnancy lasted two to five years. At the beginning of this century Sheikh Muḥammad Rashīd Riḍā (d. 1935), troubled by the contradiction between the duration of pregnancy as recognized by medicine and by the Sharīʿa, reached the following conclusion: If the duration of pregnancy, followed by breast-feeding, amounts to 30 months, as stated in Qur'an 46,15, and the breast-feeding period of "two full years" (*ḥawlayn kāmilayn*) (Qur'an 2,233) is subtracted from this, then pregnancy varies between a minimum of six months and a maximum of nine.[2]

Riḍā obviously wished to remove all differences between Muslim believers and scientific truth, hence he encouraged Muslims to embrace the findings of medicine. He also endeavored to refute Western accusations that Islamic belief was responsible for the backwardness of Muslims and their societies.

The criminal aspect of abortion

The questions if abortion is a criminal act or at what point during the pregnancy an abortion becomes a criminal act depend on the answers to other related questions: At what stage does the fetus become a human being according to the Sharīʿa? Does it matter whether the fetus at the moment of abortion is alive or dead? Can premeditated abortion be equated with either *wa'd* (infanticide) or *ʿazl* (*coitus interruptus*), two methods which Islamic law has recognized and spoken of lengthily since the Middle Ages in connection with avoidance of producing offspring.

The muftīs usually agree that *for certain specific reasons* abortions may take place during the first four months or 120 days of the pregnancy. Subsequent to this, abortions are permitted only to save the mother from a life-threatening health condition.[3]

---

[2] *Fatāwā Rashīd Riḍa*, 1st edition, Beirut 1970, v. 3, p. 836 (*Al-Manār* 12, 1909).

[3] ʿAbd Al-Ḥalīm Maḥmūd, *Al-Fatāwā*, Cairo 1986, v. 2, p. 238. Al-Shaʿrāwī is quoted in *Al-Ḥaqīqa*, October 12, 1991, p. 7.

The first 120 days cover three 40-day stages: the *nuṭfa* (a drop of seed), the *ʿalaqa* (a blood clot) and the *muḍgha* (a little lump of flesh) (based on Qur'an 22,5; 23,14). After 120 days, the angel responsible for ensoulment inspires the spirit into the fetus and it becomes a "real person".

In one *fatwa* violence against a fetus less than 120 days old was compared to the crushing of a date-stone. It had equal chances of developing into a palm tree or of rotting in the ground. Does that mean that whoever cracks a date-stone actually uproots a palm-tree[4] was the *muftī*'s question?

The metaphor conveys a clear message: the development of all fetuses is in two stages. Only after having moved into the second stage, i.e. after ensoulment, is the fetus considered "a person" according to the Sharīʿa. This has implications for the issue of punishment for a premeditated abortion: if the abortion is performed after 120 days of pregnancy it is considered a crime against a person, and *diya* (blood money) for the dead person is due if the fetus was still alive at the moment of abortion, and died only later. However, if the fetus was aborted dead, a *ghurra* is due.[5] *Ghurra* according to the Sharīʿa is the equivalent of a male or female slave and its monetary value is 50 dinars, or 600 dirhams, or five camels or 100 sheep. On average the *ghurra* is about 5% of the value of *diya*. The *ghurra* should be paid out by the *ʿāqila* (blood group) to the mother, because the fetus is perceived as one of her organs. Some even claim that after 120 days of pregnancy the fetus can be inherited by its heirs, and if no heirs can be found, then the mother inherits alone.[6] The *ghurra* has to be multiplied according to the number of aborted fetuses. If the one responsible for the abortion is proved to have acted with evil intent, some scholars even require the full amount of *diya* due in the case of an intentional homicide.[7]

---

[4] Al-Shaʿrāwī, *Al-Fatāwā*, Cairo n.d., v. 3, pp. 26-27; ʿAṭiyya Ṣaqr, "hal yajūz isqāṭ al-janīn fī ayy shahr min shuhūr al-ḥaml", *Al-Ahrām*, September 27, 1985, p. 3; Jād Al-Ḥaqq ʿAlī Jād Al-Ḥaqq, "hal yajūz ijhāḍ al-janīn al-mushawwah ? mā hiya al-aʿdhār al-mubīḥa lilijhāḍ ? hal yajūz al-taʿqīm?", *Al-Ahrām*, February 6, 1981, p. 9.

[5] Maḥmūd Shaltūt, "isqāṭ al-ḥaml", in: *Al-Fatāwā*, 3rd edition, Cairo 1966.

[6] Aḥmad Fatḥī Al-Bahansī, *Al-Qiṣāṣ fī Al-Fiqh Al-Islāmī*, Cairo 1964, pp. 99-107; Dr. ʿAlī Aḥmad Marʿī, *Al-Qiṣāṣ wal-Ḥudūd fī Al-Fiqh Al-Islāmī*, 2nd edition, Beirut 1982, pp. 46-47.

[7] Dr. ʿAlī Aḥmad Marʿī, ibid.

However, "when the mother herself takes a medicine to abort the fetus, or hurts her vagina so that the fetus is aborted" she may not inherit the *ghurra* on behalf of the fetus. She is the killer, and a killer does not inherit. On the other hand, "if she procures an abortion with her husband's permission, no *ghurra* is due, as no crime is involved." Some scholars add that even in such a case the mother still has to free a slave for compensation, since the spirit has already been inspired into the fetus.[8]

Attempts to lessen the crime involved with an abortion of a fetus younger than 120 days rely on an analogy between an abortion at the first stage of pregnancy and *ʿazl* (in which case pregnancy is prevented from the outset). But *ʿazl* is not a simple case in Islamic law, and scholars are not unanimous regarding its legitimacy. The Shāfiʿīs, for example, consider *ʿazl* undesirable (*makrūh*) Ḥanafīs, Zaydīs and Shiʿīs consider *ʿazl* permissible only if the wife approves (*mubāḥ*) the Ḥanbalīs consider it undesirable, or permissible only with the wife's approval. Mālikīs range between those labeling *ʿazl* "undesirable", and those labeling it "forbidden" (*ḥarām*). Some legal scholars consider *ʿazl* similar to *wa'd khafiyy* (disguised infanticide), hence they declare it "forbidden".[9]

Despite the absence of scholars' unanimity regarding its legitimacy, *ʿazl* became a point of departure and comparison. Based on the majority of scholars who did not reject *ʿazl* completely, it became a precedent for all contraceptives. Moreover, in 1953 the *fatwa* committee at Al-Azhar permitted the temporary use of contraceptives, referring to the Shāfiʿī approach to *ʿazl*. The Chief Muftī of Egypt, Sheikh ʿAbd Al-Majīd Salīm (d. 1954), legitimized contraceptives relying on the Ḥanafī view of *ʿazl*. Contraceptives were similarly permitted also by Sheikh Ḥasan Ma'mūn, the head of Al-Azhar mosque (1964-1969), Sheikh Aḥmad Ibrāhīm, chairman of the faculty of law at Cairo University,[10] and by Sheikh ʿAbd Allah Al-Qalqīlī of Jordan, in 1964.[11] By contrast, Sheik Al-Azhar ʿAbd Al-Ḥalīm Maḥmūd (1973-1978) objected to *ʿazl* and explained that *ʿazl* was historically legitimized to

---

[8] Aḥmad Fatḥī Al-Bahansī, *Al-Qiṣāṣ fī Al-Fiqh Al-Islāmī*, p. 107.

[9] Muḥammad Salām Madkūr, *Naẓrat Al-Islām ilā Tanẓīm Al-Nasl*, Cairo 1965.

[10] Ibid., pp. 81-85.

[11] Quoted in Olivia Schieffelin (ed.), *Muslim Attitudes toward Family Planning*, The Population Council Inc., New York 1967, pp. 3-5.

prevent the impregnation of female slaves, but it did not apply to free Muslim women.[12]

In practice, the majority of scholars tend to legitimize *ʿazl* and consequently contemporary contraceptives such as birth control pills, the condom, the IUD and the diaphragm.[13] We found, though, strong opposition to "the English shot" or the testosterone injection, which reduces sperm activity in males. Apparently, attempts have been made in Egypt to promote the use of the shot. Men are therefore warned not to use it, because it could lead to swelling of the prostate, urine retention and even to cancer of the prostate. Moreover, it should be viewed as another Western plot against Islam.[14] The question to be asked is if abortions will also be considered by these scholars as a means of preventing pregnancy and hence, can abortion win legitimacy with the relative ease that contraceptives have done so.

The present Sheikh Al-Azhar, Jād Al-Ḥaqq ʿAlī Jād Al-Ḥaqq indeed considered abortions during the first 120 days of pregnancy as means of family planning.[15] But most religious scholars have clearly differentiated between *ʿazl* and *ijhāḍ* or *saqṭ*. Al-Ghazzālī and the Ḥanbalī Ibn Rajab already in the Middle Ages viewed *ijhāḍ* as equivalent of *waʾd,* because both involved the enactment of violence against *mawjūd ḥāṣil* (an existing presence).[16] The Mālikīs prohibit the uprooting of the developing seed from the womb even before it reaches 40 days of age, all the more after the ensoulment. The Shāfiʿīs still debate whether destruction of the seed before 40 days have elapsed is to be considered *saqṭ* (abortion) or *waʾd* (infanticide).[17]

All in all it seems that comparing the termination of pregnancy by abortion to avoiding pregnancy by *coitus interruptus* is impossible, because in abortions an "existing presence" is involved, while in *coitus interruptus* it is not. If the legitimacy of *coitus interruptus* has

---

[12] *Fatāwā ʿAbd Al-Ḥalīm Maḥmūd*, 2nd edition, Cairo 1986, v. 2, pp. 481-484. Also Sheikh ʿAlī ʿAbd Al-Raḥīm, in: *Majallat Al-Tawḥīd*, Ramadan 1407, No. 9, pp. 28-29.

[13] For a comprehensive explanation of the study of the status of *ʿazl* in Islamic law see Basim F. Musallam, "Why Islam Permitted Birth Control", in: *Arab Studies Quarterly*, No. 2, Spring 1981, pp. 181-197.

[14] *Al-Nūr*, March 14, 1990, p. 3 (*muftī* Maḥmūd ʿAbd Al-Wahhāb Fāyid).

[15] *Al-Fatāwā Al-Islāmiyya*, v. 9, 1983. The original date of the *fatwā* is February 11, 1979.

[16] Dr. Muḥammad ʿAlī Al-Bār, *Khalq Al-Insān bayna Al-Ṭibb wal-Qurʾān*, p. 219.

[17] Jād Al-Ḥaqq ʿAlī Jād Al-Ḥaqq, "ḥukm al-ijhāḍ", in: *Al-Fatāwā Al-Islāmiyya*, v. 9, 1983, pp. 3093-3109. The *fatwā*'s original date is December 4, 1980.

long been the subject of discussion, abortions, where a *mawjūd ḥāsil* is indeed destroyed, are bound to provoke a much fiercer debate. Therefore, a unified legal verdict of most scholars, in favor of abortions, is not likely to be achieved in the near future.

In this regard it is interesting to note that Sheikh Ḥasan Ma'mūn prohibited the burning of "children born via abortions", as was apparently the practice in several Egyptian hospitals in order to erase all human evidence from the fetuses. He insisted that the aborted fetus must be washed (*ghusl*) and wrapped in cloth, then buried according to Sharʿī instructions. The aborted fetus deserved to die like a Muslim.[18] Sheikh Ma'mūn did not specify the exact age of a fetus for whom a full Sharʿī burial is due. Life is thus sanctified from its very early stages. Even during the first four months of pregnancy abortions are not a desired procedure, unless a reliable Muslim physician testifies that there is no alternative.[19]

Cases in which abortions are permitted

Most religious scholars are unanimous about the necessity to abort the fetus if the mother's life is endangered by it. The mother's life in such a case is never to be sacrificed to save the fetus.[20] The Egyptian law considers abortion as *junḥa* (a misdemeanor); it sometimes even becomes a *jināya* (felony), but "punishment is not due if necessity to save the life of the mother can be proved."[21]

Poverty or a low standard of living have long been debated regarding their constituting a just reason to perform abortions and/or to control the number of children per family. Those who refuse to take the economic factor in consideration often resort to the fatalistic saying

---

[18] *Al-Fatāwā Al-Islāmiyya*, v. 7, p. 2524. The *fatwā* was issued on November 8, 1955.

[19] ʿAbd Al-Ḥamīd Al-Sayyid Shāhīn (representing the Fatwa Committee in Al-Azhar), *Majallat Al-Azhar*, May 1983, pp. 1144.

[20] Maḥmūd Shaltūt, *Al-Fatāwā*, "isqāṭ al-ḥaml" Sheikh Aḥmad Haraydī, *Al-Fatāwā Al-Islāmiyya*, v. 7, pp. 2573-2574 (The *fatwā* was issued on August 26, 1968); ʿAbd Al-Ḥalīm Maḥmūd, *Al-Fatāwā*, v. 2, pp. 254; 284-285; ʿAbd Al-Ḥamīd Al-Sayyid Shāhīn, *Majallat Al-Azhar*, May 1983, pp. 1144; Jād Al-Ḥaqq ʿAli Jād Al-Ḥaqq, *Al-Daʿwa*, April 1985, p. 47; Sheikh Ḥasan Ma'mūn, *Al-Fatāwā Al-Islāmiyya*, v. 2, pp. 2546-2547 (The *fatwā* was issued on June 14, 1985).

[21] *Al-Iʿtiṣām*, November-December 1985, p. 21. According to Ghanem Isam, *Islamic Medical Jurisprudence*, London 1982, p. 60, in Kuwait in 1982 abortion was authorized if the mother's health would otherwise be seriously endangered.

that "God's table is wide", meaning that God will provide enough food for all His creatures.[22] Whoever doubts God's ability to do this has lost faith in God.[23]

Those rejecting economic considerations also present, as examples of the possible realization of the above optimistic promise, the lands of Alaska and Finland, rich in natural resources that have not yet been fully exploited for the benefit of mankind; there are many other such places, they claim.[24] Poverty or riches are anyhow temporary conditions which may not last long, while marriage and childbearing are two of the obligations of the divinely ordained Sharīʿa. Thus, whoever supports *ijhāḍ* opposes the will of the Supreme Legislator, Allah.[25]

On the other hand, we hear from Pakistani scholars in particular, but not exclusively, that the Qur'an pronounces its preference for the small family.[26] Children are a testing experience (*fitna*) for their parents (8,28; 64,15), and the parents may therefore avoid repeating it if they wish. Parents should not undertake excessive hardships incurred by raising children (Qur'an 2,233),[27] and quality is more important than quantity.[28] Quality is often translated as the ability to provide proper education for one's children. On December 29, 1980 Sheikh

---

[22] Maḥmūd Shaltūt, *Al-Fatāwa*, pp. 293-297; *Liwā' Al-Islām*, January 1991, pp. 54-55 (Dr. ʿAbd Al-Ghaffār ʿAzīz).

[23] Sheikh ʿAlī ʿAbd Al-Raḥīm, *Majallat Al-Tawḥīd*, pp. 28-29.

[24] M. Mazheruddin Siddiqi, *Women in Islam*, 7th edition, Lahore 1975, p. 201; ʿAbd Al-Ḥalīm Maḥmūd, *Al-Fatāwā*, v. 2, p. 254. Mohammad Samiullah mentions in the same spirit "Canada, New Zealand and Australia", "Islam and Birth Control", in: *Universal Message*, (Karachi) 1983, 5 (7), pp. 15-19.

[25] Sheikh Ḥasan Ma'mūn, "taḥdīd al-nasl wakhashyat al-faqr", in: *Al-Fatāwā Al-Islāmiyya*, v. 7, pp. 2546-2547. The *fatwā* was issued on June 14, 1985.

[26] Tahir Mahmood, *Family Planning: The Muslim Viewpoint*, New Delhi 1977, p. 13.

[27] Tahir Mahmood, *Family Planning: The Muslim Viewpoint*, p. 11; Abdel R. Omran, "Islam and Fertility Control", in: *Egypt: Population Problems and Prospects*, University of North Carolina 1973, pp. 165-180; Mahmud Zayid, "Family Planning in Islam", in: *People*, 1979, 6 (4), pp. 8-10.

[28] M. Saleem, "Ethical Justification of Family Planning", in: *Islamic Studies Journal*, Pakistan, Islamic Research Institute, September 1969, v. 8, no. 3, pp. 253-261; Abdel R. Omran, "Islam and Fertility Control", p. 169.

Arguments in favor of quantity are usually of the national-military kind. In Egypt, for example, in the early 1980s, several voices attributed the 1967 defeat to the numeric inferiority of the Egyptian people, hypothesizing that the Jews would not have won the war, had the population of Sinai been larger. See: ʿAbd al-Ḥalīm Maḥmūd, *Fatāwā*, v. 2, pp. 481-484; Rivka Yadlin, *Dyokan Mitzrī* (Hebrew), Jerusalem 1986, pp. 99-100, quoting *Al-Shaʿb* of June 15, 1982.

Jād Al-Ḥaqq ruled in favor of family planning through extending the periods between pregnancies, with the aim of providing a good education for all the children in the family.[29]

It should be recalled that the demographic pressure to limit the size of the family in certain Muslim societies must still withstand the trial of Sharʿī ethics.[30] Family planning has indeed become more tolerable to more religious scholars,[31] but none has yet clearly included abortions as a recommended method of achieving the goal of "the planned family".

The Qur'an and Hadith allow the prevention and even termination of pregnancy if the mother is still breast-feeding. The living child has priority over a fetus still in the womb to receive the nutritious mother's milk. It is believed that the offspring is thus protected from weakness and emaciation.[32] Sheikh Aḥmad Haraydī further restricts the justification for abortions in circumstances of *irḍāʿ* (breast-feeding) to cases where the father is financially unable to hire a wet-nurse to feed the baby instead of the pregnant mother.[33] This is to support those who claim that economic difficulties may be weighed in deciding on abortions.

Another aspect is the abortion of physically or mentally distorted fetuses, whose defects nowadays can be identified while still in womb. In Kuweit in 1982 the abortion of such fetuses was sanctioned if the defect was incurable.[34] Sheikh Shaltūt recommended that parents with genetic diseases control and limit the number of pregnancies, but he did not signify abortion as the means for this.[35] Sheikh ʿAbd Al-Ḥalīm Maḥmud did likewise.[36] Sheikh ʿAbd Al-Ḥamīd Shāhīn permitted the abortion of a defective fetus only during the first

---

[29] *Al-Fatāwā Al-Islāmiyya*, v. 9, pp. 3110-3115.

[30] In *Al-Nūr*, June 28, 1989 one finds cynical criticism of the Minister of Information of Egypt for allocating 70% of broadcasting time on radio and television for family planning.

[31] Dr. Maḥmūd Basyūnī, in: *Al-Liwāʾ Al-Islāmī*, September 5, 1991, p. 17.

[32] Maḥmūd Shaltūt, *Al-Fatāwā*, pp. 293-297; *Al-Nūr*, July 10, 1991, p. 7; *Al-Liwāʾ Al-Islāmī*, March 8, 1990, p. 6.

[33] *Al-Fatāwā Al-Islāmiyya*, v. 7, pp. 2573-2574. The *fatwā* was issued on August 26, 1968.

[34] Ghanem Isam, *Islamic Medical Jurisprudence*, p. 60.

[35] *Al-Fatāwā*, pp. 293-297. The same is true for Sheikh ʿAbd Allah Abū ʿĪd, in: *Al-Liwāʾ Al-Islāmī*, March 8, 1990, p. 6.

[36] *Al-Fatāwā*, v. 2, p. 254.

three months of pregnancy.[37] Jād Al-Ḥaqq ʿAlī Jād Al-Ḥaqq extended the permission to abort a defective fetus to the first 120 days of pregnancy. However, not every defect was considered by him as justifying an abortion. He explained that blindness, for example, or the absence of a hand, were indeed handicaps, but those suffering from such handicaps may still lead a normal life, hence no pretext for an abortion existed. He emphasized that today especially, with the availability of advanced techniques to assist handicapped people, many of them could live a "normal life". After 120 days of pregnancy the Sharīʿa recognizes no legitimate reason to abort a defective fetus.[38]

One strongly senses the scholars' fear of people playing "God" and taking the life of a defective fetus for the sole convenience of the parents. It is often suggested that the handicapped themselves may be happy in their lives, and it is only the outsider who reads misery into their situation. For the same reason, it is forbidden to abort fetuses that are the outcome of rape or adultery.[39] In these cases the killing of the fetus exacerbates the sin already committed in its creation. Besides, the fetus as a living being has a right to exist regardless of the circumstances in which it was conceived.

It seems safe to summarize the Islamic view of abortions with the words of Muṣṭafā Al-Zarqāʾ and Muḥammad Madkūr, "allowed with an excuse, and disliked without one".[40] To be more accurate, it is allowed during the first four months of pregnancy if the mother's health so requires, or when it is absolutely confirmed that the fetus is defective to a degree that it will never develop to live a dignified normal life. In other conditions, such as a breast-feeding mother or an economically destitute family, religious scholars are not unanimous about their validity in justifying an abortion.

Another question arising from the subject of abortion is if women, who due to failing health undergo recurring abortions, may resort to a more drastic measure such as sterilization, in order to avoid the preg-

[37] *Majallat Al-Azhar*, February-March 1983.

[38] *Al-Fatāwā Al-Islāmiyya*, v. 9, pp. 3093-3109 (The *fatwā* was issued on December 4, 1980); *Al-Nūr*, April 17, 1991, p. 3.

[39] *Liwāʾ Al-Islām*, April 6, 1989, p. 55; *Al-Jumʿa*, September-October 1989, p. 20; Dr. ʿAlī Al-Sālūs, *Al-Ḥaqīqa*, June 29, 1991, p. 7; Sheikh Muḥammad ʿAbd Allah Al-Khaṭīb, in: *Al-Nūr*, May 10, 1989.

[40] Quoted in Mahmud Zayid, "Family Planning in Islam". This is also the view of Sheikhs ʿAbd Allah b. Bāz, Muḥammad b. ʿAthimīn, ʿAbd Allah b. Jabarīn, in: *Fatāwā Islāmiyya li Majmūʿa min Al-Ulamāʾ Al-Afāḍil*, 1st edition, Beirut 1988, v. 3, pp. 186-187.

nancies and the subsequent abortions. Generally speaking the Sharīʿa is against sterilization as it is against all procedures that destroy the ability to conceive. These are equated to murder.[41] Recently, Sheikh Al-Shaʿrāwī prohibited sterilization and tying the tubes, even in a woman whose womb had almost ruptured as a result of the recurring Caesarian sections she had undergone.[42] The objection to sterilization is always based on the possible future regret of the mother, or on her possible future renewed desire to conceive. The main problem is seen to be the irreversibility of sterilization, *not* the pure ethical call to refrain from disfiguring bodily organs, for example.

Yet this leaves room for suggestions by several Pakistani scholars that vasectomy in men and tubectomy in women, if reversible, should be viewed as one more variation of the legitimate *ʿazl*.[43] Analogously, if *ʿazl* ever justifies abortions, sterilizations will also be considered substitutes for abortions. It is for medical research to determine the reversibility/irreversibility of vasectomy/tubectomy. From the ethical point of view, however, there seem to be less objections to operations involving sterilization than to simple operations such as nose or breast reconstruction, which also involve some change in God's creation. It seems that demographic pressure is at least partially the key to understanding this dichotomy.

Sometimes a political aspect is added to the opposition to the sterilization method: it is described as a Western plot against Muslims, which already began at the time when the West colonized the Islamic world. This plot, it is explained, aims to destroy the Muslim population and at the same time to advance the sale of Western drugs and medical devices for commercial gain at the expense of Muslims.[44]

Even scholars who view sterilization as the worst of all evils, legitimize total sterilization when the physician is confident that a mental or a genetic disease will be transferred to all the fetuses of a particular couple.[45]

---

[41] Jād Al-Ḥaqq ʿAli Jād Al-Ḥaqq, *Al-Fatāwā Al-Islāmiyya*, v. 9, pp. 3110-3115, dated December 29, 1980, and also v. 9, pp. 3093-3109, dated December 4, 1980.

[42] Al-Shaʿrāwī, *Al-Fatāwā*, Cairo n.d., v. 3, p. 29.

[43] Tahir Mahmood, *Family Planning: The Muslim Viewpoint*, p. 98.

[44] Mohammad Samiullah, "Islam and Birth Control".

[45] Muḥammad Salām Madkūr, *Naẓrat Al-Islām ilā Tanẓīm Al-Nasl*, p. 94; ʿAbd Allah Al-Mushidd in *Al-Nūr*, September 27, 1989, p. 8.

The doctor's liability

Any doctor who performs an abortion must be a devout Muslim. He must also attest prior to the abortion that the fetus poses a threat to the mother's life, or that it is defective. However, if it is the mother who chooses to abort, after the doctor has explained to her all the medical alternatives, the doctor is not held liable.[46] If the abortion is performed for a reason other than the protection of the mother's life, the ethical approach is, as pronounced by the Azhar Fatāwā Committee: "Wages earned for a forbidden act are an illegitimate income, which is therefore not suited to be considered as an enjoyable property."[47] In other words, the doctor who made the profit may not treat it as his own or as legitimate income which may be used for personal or religious purposes. It is quite possible that this statement applies also to the doctor who performs sterilizing surgery.

According to the Egyptian law, at the very least, an abortion is a "misdemeanor", but if performed by a doctor, a surgeon or a pharmacist, it becomes a "felony". Based on this, the fundamentalist Egyptian magazine *Al-I'tiṣām* declared all abortions to be essentially prohibited.[48] This attitude is harmful to women, but not only to them, because many doctors may become reluctant to perform abortions in order to escape criminal charges; desperate women are thus forced into the unskilled hands of second-rate medical professionals, or of non-professionals altogether. The liability of the Muslim physician is thus twofold: to treat the medical case, but also to defend the Shar'ī guidelines and ensure that neither doctors nor patients transgress them.

Despite the scientific progress in the field of abortions, and their relative safety, in permitting abortions contemporary muftīs are still as cautious as their colleagues were at the beginning of the century or in the 1940s and 1950s. They all believed that a mass grant of abortions, either for the sake of family planning or for other *unrequired* conditions, endangers the nature of the relationships between men and women as preached by the Sharī'a. The promiscuity that has led to the

---

46 Jād Al-Ḥaqq 'Alī Jād Al-Ḥaqq in *Al-Ahrām*, February 6, 1981.

47 *Majallat Al-Azhar*, November 1981, p. 174.

48 *Al-I'tiṣām*, p. 21; Jād Al-Ḥaqq 'Alī Jād Al-Ḥaqq, in a *fatwā* dated December 4, 1980, which was published in *Al-Fatāwā Al-Islāmīyya*, v. 9, 1983, pp. 3093-3109, also says that the Egyptian law, in "penal code" 260-264 speaks of abortions, even if performed with the woman's consent and by a licenced doctor, as felonies, unless the woman's life was at risk.

spread of abortions in the West is perceived as the biggest enemy of a stable marriage, which the Sharīʿa, via the prohibition of *zinā* (fornication) and of easy divorce, wishes to protect.

Governmentally oriented as well as fundamentalist muftīs are unanimous about the need to permit abortions only in certain individual cases, and not to permit it in principle. They all view premeditated abortions, and some even regard family planning, as attempts to pretend that it is in the power of human beings to control procreation, thus ignoring the fact that only God can create!

Still, the numerous questions regarding abortions that we have encountered clearly indicate the popular interest in it and probably also its frequent occurrence in reality.[49]

---

[49] A shrinking percentage of population growth in Egypt, compared with the 1950s, is currently attributed to the increasing use of all kinds of birth control devices, abortions being no exception. See: A. Chris Eccel, *Egypt Islam and Social Change: Al-Azhar in Conflict and Accommodation*, Beirut 1984, pp. 397-398.

CHAPTER THREE

ARTIFICIAL INSEMINATION

Islamic law emphasizes the importance of fertility in both members of a married couple and their ability to bear children as the foundation of a healthy and successful marriage.

The Prophet's encouragement to prefer to marry a fertile woman (*walūd*), who may not be so pretty, to a beautiful respectful woman who is sterile[1] well conveys this message. Not only women are addressed in regard to fertility. In the Hadith we find that a sterile man (*ʿaqīm*) is reproached by the Prophet for not informing his wife prior to their marriage that he was incapable of begetting children. The Prophet instructed the man (*akhbirhā wakhayyirhā*) "let her know and consequently let her choose!"[2] The woman was legally justified on the basis of this information, to refuse to marry the sterile man. Every woman is entitled to a productive marriage, and the law strongly defends this right.

Although marriage in Islamic law is not perceived only as a means for reproduction, and although the sexual relations between husband and wife are not believed to be merely for reproductive purposes, the bearing of mutual, legitimate children is nevertheless a desired and expected outcome of any Sharʿi marriage.

Since Islamic law recognizes no other way of obtaining children than by bearing them, especially since adoption is completely forbidden in Islamic law (*lā tabannī fī Al-Islām*), it is not surprising that infertile Muslim couples have become highly interested in artificial insemination as a means of helping them to produce the desired child.

In recent years artificial insemination has acquired a variety of forms, including test-tube babies and surrogate mothers in various contractual agreements with infertile couples, as well as the simpler methods. All these have provided new hope to childless couples all over the world. As will be shown below, some of these techniques

---

[1] *Sunan Al-Nasāʾī*, Cairo 1964, v. 6, pp. 65-66.

[2] *Muṣannaf ʿAbd Al-Razzāq*, 1st edition, Lebanon 1972, v. 6, p. 162: "Bāb Al-Rajul Al-ʿAqīm".

have not been accepted smoothly even in the West—all the less in societies still guided by strong religious ethics such as the Islamic.

The public learned of the complexities involved in artificial insemination through the publicity incurred by the court case of Baby M (born March 27, 1986 in the USA). This case involved the artificial insemination of a surrogate mother (Mrs. Whitehead) from a biological father (Mr. Stern), and also the role of the surrogate mother who after giving birth was supposed to have handed over the baby to the infertile couple, (Mr. and Mrs. Stern) in return for a large sum of money agreed upon in the contract. The baby further had to be legally adopted by the biological father's wife (Mrs. Stern) in order to realize her and her husband's custody over it.

Problems arose when Mrs. Whitehead regretted her previous agreement to give up the baby, and refused to fulfill her part of the contract. The legal battle over Baby M started. It took the court 32 sessions to decide the issue. The verdict was against the validity of the contract, and for custody by the Sterns. It also allowed the biological mother visitation rights.

The details of the trial are beyond the scope of our topic. The significance of the case, however, is that it sheds light on a new reproductive method and the ethical problems it entails. These should encourage scientists to focus on developing alternative reproductive methods which may offer the same welcome results, but with less distress to the parties involved.[3]

Contemporary Muslim jurists, without referring to the Baby M case in particular, seem to be well acquainted with the various forms of artificial insemination, and they assess them ethically.

Before turning to these various forms, two basic tenets, which concern all forms of artificial insemination in their Islamic application, must be stressed:

a. Islamic law acknowledges that pregnancy can sometimes occur other than by direct sexual contact, i.e., without penetration. The child born through indirect/artificial insemination is therefore legitimate. In medieval Islamic law it was recognized that the woman may herself insert into her vagina semen which she believed was her husband's. If it later transpired that it was not, she

---

[3] A detailed account and analysis of the Baby M case can be found in Tom L. Beauchamp and LeRoy Walters (eds.), *Contemporary Issues in Bioethics*, 3rd edition, USA 1989, pp. 502-513.

would have to practice *'idda*—a waiting period intended to verify that she was not pregnant. The case was equated with that of *al-mawṭū'a bishubha* (a woman who was by mistake sexually taken by a man other than her husband),[4] who too was not held responsible for the results of the error. In other words, both cases are proof that indirect insemination as a general method is not dismissed or spurned.

b. Bringing about pregnancy by means other than direct sexual contact is not perceived as interference in the Creator's acts, nor as contesting God's wish and decree. On the contrary: Islam desires that mankind be happy. Artificial insemination is made possible through knowledge which God has provided. Medicine alone is not capable of producing an egg or semen. It can only improve the way the two unite, after God has created them.[5] Therefore, only the ignorant may think that artificial insemination is a unique achievement of science. If God had not so wished, artificial insemination would not have succeeded. Proof for this is that artificial inseminations are never 100 percent successful. Likewise contraception: not every use of contraceptives prevents conception, just as not every couple who practice intercourse and wish to bear children succeed. The gap between the expected and the realized represents the true power of God.

Both tenets lead to the acceptability of artificial insemination as a general technique by Muslim jurists.

Sheikh Al-Azhar Jād Al-Ḥaqq enumerated all the occurrences which he thought came under the general method of artificial insemination:[6]

a. the husband's sperm is artificially transferred to his wife while they live together.
b. the sperm of a different man is transferred to a married woman whose husband has no sperm, or whose sperm is sterile.
c. the husband's sperm is used to fertilize the ovum of another woman; the fertilized ovum is then transferred to the uterus of his wife, who has no ova.

---

4 Maḥmūd Shaltūt, *Al-Fatāwā*, 2nd edition, Cairo 1966, pp. 325-326.

5 "ṭifl al-anābīb wal-talqiḥ al-ṣinā'ī", in: *Al-Liwā' Al-Islāmī*, April 2, 1987, p. 21.

6 His *fatwā* is dated March 23, 1980, and was published in *Al-Fatāwā Al-Islāmiyya*, v. 9, pp. 3213-3228.

d. the ovum of the wife is fertilized by her husband's sperm outside the uterus (in vitro) and then:
   1. it is returned to the wife's uterus, or
   2. deposited in the uterus of a suitable animal and later returned to the wife's uterus.

Case (a) is used when the woman has anatomical obstacles to becoming pregnant, such as absence or blockage of the fallopian tubes, but both she and her husband are fertile.

Case (b) is a typical solution for infertile husbands and fertile wives. Sperm banks have been established mainly to solve such problems.

Case (c) is the solution for women who do not ovulate but are otherwise capable of carrying a full-term pregnancy.

Case (d1) is the now common test-tube babies, i.e., when impregnation cannot occur in a womb but having occurred elsewhere, it can be fostered by it. Case (d2) is when the pregnancy and its first stages are intolerable to the woman's body, and a longer incubation in another womb is required.

Dr. Yūsuf Al-Qirḍāwī hypothesizes on another method, which he claims has not yet been tried but is medically possible. In this method, the wife's ovum and the husband's sperm are both deposited in the body of another woman because the wife for some reason has no womb. This is actually the transplant of a fetus (*shatl al-janīn*). The "hired womb" will carry the baby full term until delivery, whereupon it will be handed over to its biological parents. Al-Qirḍāwī speculates that beautiful or very wealthy women might misuse this method to have children without investing any effort and without impairing their beauty, etc.[7] Theoretically, with such a method a wealthy woman can "spread" her eggs among several women's "hired wombs" simultaneously, in order to produce many children in a short period.

Needless to say, Al-Qirḍāwī 's view of this method is clearly derogatory. He suggests that the problems that this method is supposed to solve would be better answered through a womb transplant.[8] This, as far as we know, has never yet been tried.

Case (a), in which the husband's sperm is artificially transferred to his wife, is permitted by most Muslim legalists. However, if such a transfer is not made exclusively between the married couple, *zinā*

---

[7] "shatl al-janīn", in: *Fatāwā Muʿāṣira*, 3rd edition, Kuwait 1987, pp. 562-563.

[8] Ibid.

(fornication) is detected and due punishment has to be inflicted. In addition, irreversible damage is caused to the status of a child born through this procedure. Artificial insemination from a different man is viewed as worse than adoption (*tabannī*), hence definitely forbidden.[9]

However, based on Shaltūts *fatwā*, we also found another opinion which completely prohibited all artificial inseminations,[10] based on the experience of Western countries, in which the principle of husband to wife inseminations only, is not strictly observed.

Recently, based on several court decisions in Western countries, it has been permitted for a wife to use her husband's sperm after his death. The scientific ability to preserve semen in good condition over long periods has made this technically possible.

On November 16, 1988 Sheikh ʿAbd Allah Al-Mushidd published a *fatwā* in *Al-Nūr*, in which he allowed the wife to use the seed of her husband after his death.

Naturally, this evoked opposition among Muslim scholars. Muḥammad Muṣṭafā Shalabī, a Sharīʿa professor at the Universities of Alexandria and Beirut, demanded that the age of the wife be taken into consideration in granting her such permission, so that she will not become pregnant at an advanced age and cause a scandal. Shalabī also expressed fear lest a divorcee become pregnant during the year following the divorce, knowing that a child born within a year after death or divorce, still belongs to the *firāsh* (bed) of his father, according to all schools of Islamic law. Therefore, by bearing a child within that year the child's status is not jeopardized. Another fear which Shalabī expressed is that a widow might be tempted to become pregnant after her husband's death to revive his memory through the "remnants" he has left.

Professor Shalabī states that pregnancy in the absence of the husband (divorce or death) causes problems both to the *nasab* (geneology) of the child and to the distribution of the deceased's bequest. Artificial insemination, he concludes, is permitted only from husband to wife, as long as they maintain proper marriage relations and are both alive.[11]

---

9 "al-talqīḥ al-ṣināʿī", in: Maḥmūd Shaltūt, *Al-Fatāwā*, pp. 325-329; *Al-Iʿtiṣām*, June 1989, pp. 38-39; Sheikh Muḥammad Al-Abāṣīrī Khalīfa, "al-tawālud bil-talqīḥ al-ṣināʿī", in: *Al-Marʾa wal-Tarbiya Al-Islāmiyya*, 1st edition, Kuwait 1984, pp. 92-94; *Al-Liwāʾ Al-Islāmī*, March 1, 1990, p. 6 (*muftī* ʿAbd Al-Munṣif Maḥmūd).

10 *Al-Umma Al-Islāmiyya*, August 1985, p. 8.

11 *Al-Iʿtiṣām*, June 1989, pp. 38-39.

Cases (b) and (c) are not acceptable to Islamic law, because they involve violation of the marriage contract and the *nasab* that it normally guarantees. Further, it is claimed that cases such as (b) and (c) may create difficult psychological problems. In case (b) the wife's curiosity may be aroused as to whose semen has been inserted into her body, and she may also grow contemptuous of her sterile husband. Consequently their family will be destroyed.[12]

Case (d1) is the recently popular test-tube baby method. Most Muslim jurists permit this technique, as long as the sperm is the husband's and the ovum is the wife's.[13] No other combination is allowed. The method is permitted even if the husband has to masturbate in order to collect the seed into a vessel,[14] although Islamic law in general is not supportive of free masturbation.[15]

An exception is ʿAbd Al-Ḥalīm Maḥmūd, Sheikh Al-Azhar in 1973-1978, who prohibits all test-tube inseminations. He claims that a child born via a test-tube lacks a father and a mother, and lacks feelings and human warmth. Sheikh Maḥmūd also resorts to a demographic argument, that there is no need to add to the already over-populated world with test-tube babies.[16] He disqualifies all test-tube inseminations without differentiating between them, and without considering the humane problem of childless couples that the method is meant to address. The demographic argument was quite common in Egypt among certain circles as a means of solving its population crisis, especially in the 1960s. It was influenced then by attitudes of the political regime.[17]

---

[12] *Al-Liwāʾ Al-Islāmī*, April 2, 1987.

[13] Ibid. See also: *Al-Daʿwa*, October 1978; ʿAbd Al-Munṣif Maḥmūd, in: *Al-Liwāʾ Al-Islāmī*, March 1, 1990, p. 6, and *Al-Liwāʾ Al-Islāmī*, March 15, 1990, p. 7; Jād Al-Ḥaqq ʿAlī Jād Al-Ḥaqq in the *fatwā* dated March 23, 1980.

[14] Abul Fadl Mohsin Ebrahim, *Biomedical Issues—Islamic Perspective*, Mobeni South Africa, Islamic Medical Association of South Africa, 1988. In Jewish law, for example, the frequent resort to masturbation in the process of artificial insemination renders the process itself more questionable than it is under Islamic law.

[15] According to the Mālikīs and Shāfiʿīs, masturbation by hand is prohibited. According to the Hanafīs, it is permitted if the man is unmarried, for example, and wants to avoid fornication. Masturbation by imagining one's wife is permitted. Dr. Muḥammad Bakr Ismāʿīl, *Al-Fiqh Al- Wāḍiḥ*, Cairo 1990, v.2, pp. 231-232.

[16] "fī talqīḥ awlād al-anābīb", in: *Al-Fatāwā*, 2nd edition, Cairo 1986, v. 2, pp. 245-246.

[17] The demographic argument was often used also with regard to family planning and abortion. See our chapter on "Abortions".

The use of surrogate mothers, like that of Baby M., is utterly unthinkable to Muslim jurists. According to them, in such cases the husband is merely a minor participant in the reproductive process. A strange woman, not his wife, carries the fetus full term and acts, illegally, as his wife would in normal pregnancies. There also is the adoption which the father's wife must conduct and which adds another sin to that of fornication, as already observed.

Attempts to compare the case of Hagar and Abraham to a surrogate mother's case are strongly refuted; Hagar was given by the barren Sarah to Abraham as a second wife. Any wife is entitled to bear her husband children, and the child is then legitimate beyond doubt.[18]

One reason why artificial insemination is permitted only from husband to wife is the concern for the status of the children who are born in such a way. A child born from seed foreign to his mother (out of wedlock) is illegitimate—*walad zinā* (bastard). He belongs to his mother but not to his father, because his relation to the *firāsh* (bed) of his father is dubious. In artificial insemination other than from husband to wife, the father actually agrees to the *zinā* of his wife. This was common practice in the Jāhiliyya, known as *istibḍāʿ* (intentionally becoming pregnant not by the husband), but Islamic law prohibited it.[19]

Use of the sperm banks established to supply childless couples with fertile semen is also viewed as a disguised form of *zinā*. The only difference is that the perpetrators of *zinā* are unknown to the recipient of the sperm. These banks may tempt someone to provide beautiful women with semen of intelligent men, in an attempt to produce a better human race. This stands in clear contradiction to the original structure of the family as so strongly protected by Islamic law.[20]

Jād Al-Ḥaqq equates the child born via forbidden artificial insemination to a foundling (*laqīṭ*), who cannot be affiliated with a father, only with the mother who gave birth to him. The *laqīṭ* he adds, should

[18] Ghazala Javaid, "On Surrogate Motherhood", *Journal of the Islamic Medical Association*, (USA) 1987, 19 (3), p. 126.

[19] *Majallat Al-Azhar*, November 1981, p. 314. *Istibḍāʿ* is defined as "a type of marriage in the Jāhiliyya". A woman would approach a man sexually, only with the purpose of becoming pregnant. Her husband, who approved of it, would abstain from physical contact with her, until her pregnancy by that man was verified. See: Al-Zabīdī, *Tāj Al-ʿArūs*, Kuwait 1983, v. 20, p. 343.

[20] Jād Al-Ḥaqq in the *fatwā* dated March 23, 1980.

be treated similarly to *walad zinā*.[21] In our opinion, this equation is not apt.

It is true that the *laqīṭ* is sometimes deserted because he is also a *walad zinā*, but not always. In the case of *walad zinā* the mother is usually known. In the case of a *laqīṭ* sometimes both parents are anonymous, but based on later testimony by one of them, the *nasab* can be reaffirmed, and the *laqīṭ* can be elevated in status, unlike *walad zinā*[22]

Nevertheless, even the Shi'ite jurist Al-Ṭabāṭabā'ī, who maintained that the "child product of insemination is not the outcome of sin, and cannot be disowned of course by the mother, and is accordingly capable of inheriting from her (and vice versa)," refrained from defining the child's status vis-à-vis his mother's husband.[23] In Islamic societies, when a child's affiliation with his/her father is dubious, it practically does not matter that his/her mother is legally recognized. The child is doomed to be a social outcast.

As for the man who agrees that his wife be inseminated by another man's sperm—he loses his manly honor, and consequently deserves being classified in Islamic law as *dayyūth* (weak and despised).[24] If the wife was not aware of the forbidden insemination given to her, she is exempt from punishment. Her husband and the participating doctor, however, are not.[25]

The doctor who performs a forbidden insemination is a sinner, and his acts are defined as sins, because "When Islam prohibits something, it also prohibits the means to perform the prohibited, so that they do not become a vehicle for immersing in the prohibited."[26]

The confidentiality which naturally surrounds artificial insemination often serves as the cover for both husbands and doctors who give their consent to the method. "The "crime" is therefore hard to prove and to eradicate.

---

21 Ibid.

22 On the legal status of the *laqīṭ*, see: Sayf Al-Dīn Al- Qaffāl, *Ḥulyat Al-Ulamā' fī Ma'rifat Madhāhib Al-Fuqahā'*, Jordan 1985, v. 5, pp. 550-574.

23 Ghanem Isam, *Islamic Medical Jurisprudence*, London 1982, pp. 57-58.

24 Jād Al-Ḥaqq in a *fatwā* dated March 23, 1980. *Dayyūth* is the man who is too weak to protect his wife, and consequently lets others violate the dignity of his wife while he sees and knows. Al-Zabīdī, *Tāj Al-'Arūs*, Kuwait 1969, v. 5, p. 254.

25 *Majallat Al-Azhar*, November 1981, p. 314.

26 Jād Al-Ḥaqq in a *fatwā* dated March 23, 1980.

At least in one country, Libya, artificial inseminations have been treated severely by the law. Law no. 175 of 7 December 1972 prohibits artificial insemination. Article 403/A provides for up to ten years' imprisonment to whoever causes artificial insemination of a woman through deceit, threat or force, and five years only if the woman agrees to the procedure. Article 403/B states that a woman who agrees to artificial insemination may be sentenced to five years in prison, like her husband. The reasoning of the legislator is that these inseminations pose a threat to the preservation of a pure *nasab* (genealogy) and violate the rights of the legitimate heirs who, as a result of artificial insemination, must unexpectedly share with an outsider. The husband's consent leads to illegal results, principally the adoption of his wife's child begot by another man. Finally, artificial insemination is viewed as an interference with God's decrees.[27]

We have no way of knowing how applicable these laws are, especially to people desperate to bear a child in a society which considers bearing children a sign of prosperity and which does not welcome adoptions.

More moderate religious voices, who accommodate the "less harmful" types of artificial insemination, seem in any case to be the majority. They also appear to be more considerate of human nature.

[27] Ann Elizabeth Mayer, "Libyan Legislation in Defence of Arabo-Islamic Sexual Mores", *American Journal of Comparative Law* 1980, 28 (2), pp. 287-313.

CHAPTER FOUR

ORGAN TRANSPLANT

The first body parts that were replaced by transplantation were skin, bone, teeth, blood and the cornea. The first kidney transplant was in 1954, first liver transplant in 1960, the first heart transplant in 1967. On 17 December 1986 a great medical advance was achieved in England with the first combined transplant of heart, lungs and kidney.[1]

When these pioneering steps came to the knowledge of Muslims, religious Muslim scholars were urged to evaluate the concept of human organ transplants as well as their practical and moral implications from an Islamic point of view.

Since the 1950s, therefore, Muslim scholars and jurists have been preoccupied with the subject of transplants. The increasing number of transplants in the late 1970s and 1980s resulted in an increasing number of Muslim scholars' responsa in the 1980s and 1990s on the ethical aspects of the issue.

Human transplants, because of obvious scientific, religious and other obstacles, were not practiced in the lifetime of the Prophet,[2] nor are they mentioned in the Qur'an. Muslim jurists had to resort to the general ethical concepts that Muslims apply in all fields of life, including medicine, in their overall positive intention to allow Muslims to be healed by transplants too—the latest medical techniques. This does not mean that Muslims are now entirely free of reservations and doubts about some aspects of the transplant process. But it does mean that the jurists have recalled several acceptable Islamic dogmas and applied them to the field of transplants—using these dogmas as a legal source to legitimize transplants in lieu of the Qur'an and Sunna, which lack any reference to the topic.

Some of these dogmas are as follows:

---

[1] M. Zakaria Siddiqi, "Legal Issues in Human Organ Transplant: Indian Perspective", *Islam and Comparative Law Quarterly*, 7, 1987, pp. 144-164.

[2] Although bone transplants from animals were used to join together fractured human bones, see: Babu Sahib, Maulavi M.H., "The Islamic Point of View on Transplantation of Organs", *Islam and Comparative Law Quarterly*, 7, 1987, pp. 128-131. The author is a member of the Muslim Religious Council of Singapore.

a. Breaking the bone of the dead is equal to breaking the bone of the living, therefore, no unjustified or unnecessary harm should be done to the dead body without warranting punishment.[3] Absolutely necessary treatments are, of course, excluded from the prohibition.
b. A lesser injury (*ḍarar akhaff*) to the body of the deceased is tolerated in order to prevent the greater injury (*ḍarar ashadd*) to the living person, who may die if a transplant is not made in time.[4]
c. The particular injury (*ḍarar akhaṣṣ*) to the deceased him/herself is tolerated so as to avert the public injury (*ḍarar ʿāmm*) to the living person and his/her successors, and consequently to society at large. The latter injury will occur if transplant is not performed.[5]
d. No injury should be inflicted in order to prevent another equal injury. Therefore, there must appear to be a fairly good chance that the recipient of the organ will recover from his/her disease as a result of the transplant. Otherwise the damage caused to the donor is not justified.[6]
e. Whoever saves one life is considered to have saved humanity at large. Therefore, all efforts to save a life which possibly can be saved are legitimized; transplants, which involve injuring the body of the donor, are no exception.[7]
f. Analogously to permission granted to seek a cure through forbidden liquids, foods and impure substances (*al-tadāwī bil-muḥarram*), transplants are permitted too. The principle is that human life must be saved even at the price of violating certain religious prohibitions.[8]
g. Necessities render the prohibited permitted (*al-ḍarūrāt tubīḥ al-maḥẓūrāt*) When there is no other way to save life, forbidden

---

[3] *Muṣannaf ʿAbd Al-Razzāq*, Beirut 1970-1972, v.3, p. 444. See also a *fatwā* by Dr. Muḥammad Sayyid Ṭanṭāwī, "bayʿ al-insān liʿuḍw min aʿḍāʾihi aw al-tabarruʿ bihi", in: *Minbar Al-Islām*, June 1988, pp. 36-41.

[4] *Minbar Al-Islām*, June 1988, pp. 36-41; Sheikh Ibrāhīm Al-Yaʿqūbī, *Shifāʾ Al-Taʾrīkh wal-Adwāʾ fī Ḥukm Al-Tashrīḥ wal-Aʿḍāʾ*, 1st edition, Damascus 1986.

[5] Yaʿqūbī, ibid.

[6] Jād Al-Ḥaqq ʿAlī Jād Al-Ḥaqq, "hal yajūz naql al-aʿḍāʾ min insān mayyit ilā insān ḥayy?", *Al-Ahrām*, September 4, 1981, p. 13.

[7] First International Conference on Islamic Medicine, *Islamic Code of Medical Ethics*, Kuwait, January 1981, p. 83.

[8] Yaʿqūbī, ibid.

means become permitted; this includes the removal of organs from a dead person.[9]

h. "Seek remedy for any disease." This Prophetic saying is interpreted as "Do not neglect any measure to bring about cure, even if it requires transplants from the dead."[10]

i. The donation of body parts is a social obligation, like those classified by Islamic law as *farḍ kifāya* (a duty of a sufficient number of community members). This means that the community as a collective body is obliged to find the right organs for transplanting in its sick members. If a sick person died while awaiting a transplant, the society as a whole is held responsible for killing him/her. The medical staff in charge of the transplant procedure for this purpose represents the whole community. Once an organ for transplant has been obtained, the community regards itself exempt from seeking further cure for the recipient of the organ.[11]

The above general statements, which are so often quoted in relation to organ transplants, have furthered the willingness of Islamic medical ethics to overlook Sharʿī prohibitions when saving life is at stake. Life should be saved at any cost, and if transplants are a sort of cure so be it with them too.

The process of transplant itself, although generally accepted, still raises ethical questions, which are addressed below.

Is it permitted to donate a body part?

The usual case is that the donor him/herself, by a legal testimony or in the will, authorizes that after death a certain body part, or all the body

---

[9] Jād Al-Ḥaqq ʿAlī Jād Al-Ḥaqq "naql al-aʿḍāʾ min insān ilā ākhar", in: *Al-Fatāwā Al-Islāmiyya*, v. 10, pp. 3702-3715. He equates the principle of "the needs which justify the prohibited" with the occasional need to cut open a woman's body in order to rescue a living fetus.

[10] See for example: ʿAbd Al-Raḥmān Muḥammad Uthmān (ed.), *Sunan Al-Tirmidhī*, Al-Madīna 1964, v. 3, p. 258.

[11] *Islamic Code of Medical Ethics*, p. 81. In this source it is also mentioned that the Caliph Umar b. Al-Khaṭṭāb accused the community, one of whose members died of hunger, of killing him, and ordered them to pay ransom (*fīdya*). Similarly, the community is held responsible for the death of a person, if the community could not provide blood or organ donation for him/her. A part of the collective responsibility involves the provision of the minimal means of survival for all human beings.

may be used for transplants. It is also possible that the nearest relatives (*awliyā'*) of the deceased agree, upon request by the medical staff, to the removal of an organ from the deceased for transplant.

This stands in contradiction to the monotheistic and Islamic principle that no one owns his/her body to a degree of full ownership. The body, at most, is a deposit for a lifetime, after which it is returned to the Creator. As such, a person cannot theoretically decide what to do with his/her body or with any part of it after death. For all that, Muslim scholars have asserted that some degree of general control over the body is nevertheless given to any person. This may be interpreted at least as temporary ownership. Compelled by the desire to prevent harm to the living party (awaiting a donation), and to protect the public benefit, Muslim scholars rendered organ donations permitted and possible.[12]

Inasmuch as the body is not one's property, it is also forbidden to commit a suicide, i.e., to destroy the deposit which God entrusted with man. The donation in one's lifetime of an organ of which the human has only one (heart, liver, pancreas, etc.) is actually committing suicide, and is therefore forbidden.[13] The donation of an organ of which there are two in the body (kidneys, lungs, etc.) is viewed as a highly humanitarian and noble act.[14] Another view states that the fact that there are two similar organs does not allow us to donate one of them. They should not be treated as spare parts. If they were, why would God not have created three or more of them?[15]

The body tissues are classified as regenerative or non-regenerative. The former include skin and bone marrow, and of course blood. The latter include the majority of organs, which if amputated cannot be regenerated.[16] This information is crucial for deciding on donations in the lifetime of the donor; only donations of the regenerative type can be multiple. Non-regenerative organs can be donated once, at most, and often only after the donor's death.

---

[12] Ya'qūbī, p. 38.

[13] Babu Sahib, Moulavi M.H., "The Islamic Point of View on Transplantation of Organs".

[14] Ibid.

[15] Dr. 'Abd Al-Salām Al-Sukkarī, *Al-Nūr*, January 16, 1991, p. 5.

[16] M. Zakaria Siddiqi, "Legal Issues in Human Organ Transplant: Indian Perspective", p. 145.

Is the sanctity of the deceased's body not violated?

In cognizance of the fact that the body is not legally one's property and therefore it should be returned to God upon death in the best shape and condition, the question arises if the section of a body to remove an organ for transplant in another does not violate the sanctity of the donor's body.

The Prophet, who stated that "breaking a bone of the dead is equal to breaking a bone of a living person," emphasized the necessity of preserving the human right to be buried in one piece (unlike the pre-Islamic Arabs, who mutilated corpses of their enemies). This will also be an important issue in the chapter on postmortems.

Those who insist on the burial of the body with all its organs, rely on Qur'an 17, 36 which reads "(O man) follow not that whereof thou hast no knowledge. Lo! the hearing and the sight and the heart—of each of these it will be asked." Since on Resurrection Day the heart, hearing and sight will be questioned, they must physically be present. Therefore, the "deposit" or "trust" (*amāna*) i.e. the body, must be wholly returned to God.

One possible refutation of this claim is that the questioning will involve what one *did* with the above-mentioned faculties, and not why these faculties were not returned in full.[17] As for the "trust" itself, it was invested in a good cause; it was properly used and need not be returned at all.[18] "Donating the organ for transplantation so that the organ is given a better use, more respectful than merely being buried and allowed to be eaten by insects and worms is not prohibited in Islam."[19] In our view, this might be stretching permission to donate organs a little too far; it questions the importance of a respectable Islamic burial, which all chapters on *jināza* (burial) in Islamic legal literature so meticulously describe. Such an opinion is obviously tendentious and aimed at encouraging organ donations. In support of this opinion it is added that in the Hereafter God will find no difficulty in assembling all the organs of the deceased from wherever they may be

---

[17] Babu Sahib, Moulavi M.H., "The Islamic Point of View on Transplantation of Organs".

[18] Ibid. According to the Ḥanbalīs, the trustee is not responsible for the trust, unless he did not protect it, or over protected it and it was damaged, or unless it was lost. "Improving" the shape of the trust is excluded. See: 'Abd Al-Raḥmān Al-Jazīrī, *Al-Fiqh 'alā Al-Madhāhib Al-Arba'a*, Cairo 1990, v. 3, p. 233.

[19] Babu Sahib, Moulavi M.H., "The Islamic Point of View on Transplantation of Organs".

located, in order to resurrect him/her. Meanwhile, it is enough that the remaining organs (those which have not been transplanted) be given a dignified Islamic burial.[20]

According to another opinion, violation of the dignity of the deceased is less than the benefit in saving the life of the living, therefore the latter has priority. Besides, the dead donor will be rewarded for the donation and also gain from the fact that his/her organ outlives him/her.[21] Muslims, it is claimed, are encouraged to sacrifice their lives in *jihād* (holy war) for the sake of their people. Donation of organs for the sake of other people should also be viewed as a sacrifice made for the benefit of others, hence a noble act too.[22] The Fatāwā Committee of Egypt decreed with regard to skinning the dead for the purpose of curing burns that it is a violation of their dignity *unless* the benefit which accrues from the skinning is greater than the injury caused.[23]

How to define the moment of death?

This question is relevant for donations of organs after death. It is particularly crucial for such organs as the liver, heart, lungs, kidneys and pancreas, because these must be removed before they are deprived of the supply of oxygenated blood. This means that before the removal of such organs the body mechanism must still be operating. It naturally creates a very sensitive situation, in which death is assumed before it is diagnosed.

The USA ad hoc Committee of the Harvard Medical School approved the concept of brain death as the legal point of death.[24]

Since no technical problem exists nowadays to prolong life greatly by respirators, pacemakers and other sophisticated machines after brain damage or irreversible coma have occurred, it has been felt that the point of death has to be differently defined. The legal definition of

---

20 Ibid. See also: Ahmad, Furqan, "Organ Transplant in Islamic Law", in: *Islamic and Comparative Law Quarterly*, 7, 1987, pp. 132-136.

21 Ya'qūbī, pp. 43; 41.

22 Muḥammad Abū Shādī, in: *Majallat Al-Azhar*, April 1973, pp. 283-285.

23 *Al-Fatāwā Al-Islāmiyya*, v. 7, Cairo 1982, pp. 2505-2507: "salkh jild al-mayyit li'lāj ḥurūq al-aḥyā'".

24 *Journal of the American Medical Association*, 337, 1968. See: Ṣiddiqi, "Legal Issues in Human-Organ Transplant: Indian Perspective", p. 154; Badar Durrez, Ahmad, "Organ Transplant and the Right to Die", *Islamic and Comparative Law Quarterly*, 7, 1987, pp. 121-127 (The author is a member of the Supreme Court of India).

death—first accepted by Western medical staff—is now recognized almost everywhere.

Historically, in Islamic medicine death was diagnosed when the patient stopped breathing and his/her heart ceased beating. In the past this was useful for questions of succession and bequest. In ascent to the throne, however, the brain death of the previous ruler was recognized as the mark that a successor may take power. Hence we learn that Islamic law too differentiated between two forms of death, and identified brain death as the point when life stopped being natural and independent.[25]

For juridicial purposes, the person with brain death is considered dead. Organs may then be removed, if authorization for their removal has been properly obtained. However, if organs are removed before death has been verified, the act is defined by Islamic law as *qatl* (murder, or at least killing), or *īdhā'*[26] (causing injury), for which punishment is due or ransom has to be paid, or both. It is also forbidden to use organs of a terminally ill patient because the definition of "terminally ill" is vague, hence unaccepted legally. Miracles of recovery may still occur although the major miracles ended with the death of the Prophet.[27] Muslim jurists have to walk a very narrow path between trusting in the omnipotence of Allah who might at any moment surprise them by sending a cure to the terminally ill, and the medical observations, which, based on experience and statistics, foretell the proximity of brain-death (when organs would be allowed to be removed for transplant).

Still, medicine is often given priority and transplants are practised at the expense of belief in God's miracles. The legal justifications which accompany this choice are meant to make it easy for devout Muslims to resign to the "new" preference.

It is recommended, therefore, that more than one physician verify the death of a potential donor, and that none of the physicians who verify death are in any way connected with the future transplant of any organ taken from that particular deceased.[28] All is done to prevent personal interests in a hasty transplant entailing a criminal act against the dying person.

---

[25] Ghanem Isam, *Islamic Medical Jurisprudence*, London 1982, pp. 62-63.

[26] Ya'qūbī, p. 106.

[27] *Al-Nūr*, April 4, 1990, pp. 4-5.

[28] Badar Durrez, Ahmad, "Organ Transplant and the Right to Die", p. 123.

Who are the preferred donors, and what conditions should they fulfil?

In the first place donors should be *ḥarbīs* (members of the enemy party), because their blood is violable; or they should be people who deserve to die for a crime committed, for apostasy (*ridda*) or because they have murdered and deserve *qiṣāṣ* (death penalty).[29] Another legal opinion permits organ donations to be obtained from bodies of those sentenced to death, but after execution.[30]

This may hint that organ donation is still viewed as harmful to the dignity of the deceased. Therefore, it is suggested that donations should in the first place be sought from those who endanger Islamic society, from without or within, and from those whom Islamic law wishes to humiliate and punish. The latter have already lost their legal standing owing to misconduct. It is easier to make use of their bodies, therefore, with no need to take account of their legal status or of their families' feelings.

Only after this category of outcasts has been fully exhausted is it permitted to accept donations from others, but here too, only after the "others" have fulfilled certain essential conditions.[31]

A living person who decides to donate an organ must do so out of free will, without being morally or socially coerced and without economic pressures. This means that no advantage is taken of the donor's poverty, or that he/she has been offered a large sum of money in exchange for the organ. If the donation is not voluntary, the rights of freedom of action and of ownership are violated.[32]

The donor should ensure that the donation will not endanger his/her life or weaken him/her or cause deformation to his/her body.[33] Some suggest that a doctor must testify, prior to the donation that the donor will not be physically hurt by the donation.[34] No human being should be forced to donate an organ, even when he/she is the only possible donor on earth.[35] This too is for the purpose of preserving the

---

[29] Ya'qūbī, p. 108.

[30] Dr. Muḥammad Sayyid Ṭanṭāwī, in: *Al-Liwā' Al-Islāmī*, April 19, 1990, p. 8.

[31] Ya'qūbī, p. 108.

[32] *Islamic Code of Medical Ethics*, pp. 81; 84.

[33] Jād Al-Ḥaqq 'Alī Jād Al-Ḥaqq, in: *Al-Fatāwā Al-Islāmiyya*, v. 10, pp. 3702-3715. The *fatwā* is dated December 5, 1979. *Al-Ahrām*, January 5, 1990, p. 15 quotes Dr. 'Abd Al-Fattāḥ Al-Sheikh, the Rector of Al-Azhar University.

[34] Dr. Muḥammad Sayyid Ṭanṭāwī, in: *Minbar Al-Islām*, June 1988, pp. 36-41.

[35] Siddiqi, "Legal Issues in Human-Organ Transplant: Indian Perspective", p. 151.

body as complete as possible, because it is not fully owned, and is rather a trust which belongs to Allah, as has already been explained.

Potential donations by minors and the mentally disabled are legitimate, provided proxy consent of their guardian has been attained.[36] This is meant to eliminate the opportunities for exploitation of children and the mentally ill as suppliers of organs for transplants.[37]

Donations from people who have already died can be used on the basis of their own signed will or authorization obtained from their relatives postmortem.[38]

If the deceased has no relatives, or the relatives are unknown, the Attorney General's Office can grant permission to remove an organ for transplant.[39]

In Egypt, based on *fatāwā* no. 212 of February 14, 1959; no. 173 of February 3, 1973; no. 188 of February 5, 1974 and no. 190 of March 5, 1974, it is legally permitted to remove organs from deceased people who have no known relatives, for medical and criminal identification purposes, and also for transplants.[40] These *fatāwā* expand the guardianship of the state over people who have no relatives also to matters of transplant authorization. The state is authorized by law to act as their guardian in matters of criminal charges, financial liabilities and bequests, to mention only a few.

The modern Egyptian legislation obviously adopts existing Islamic law to the arising needs of the present. The law emphasizes that even a person with no relatives is protected from mutilation after death or physical abuse before death.

There is, however, a discrimination against those who have no relatives from those who have. This has been known in Islamic law since its formative stages. It probably originates from the centrality granted to the blood group in Islamic society over the individual.

It is permitted that the donor be a heretic (*kāfir*) and the recipient a Muslim (at least when the donation is of an eye). Heretics themselves, or their relatives, are still required to grant permission. Muslims may

[36] Ibid., p. 152.

[37] Ibid., p. 164.

[38] *Al-Ahrām*, January 5, 1990; Dr. Muḥammad Sayyid Ṭanṭāwī, in: *Minbar Al-Islām*, June 1988; Muḥammad Abū Shādī, in: *Majallat Al-Azhar*, April 1973, pp. 283-285; Ghanem Isam, "Islamic Medical Jurisprudence", in: *Medicine Science and the Law*, 1981, vol. 21, no. 4, pp 275-287.

[39] Jād Al-Ḥaqq ʿAlī Jād Al-Ḥaqq in the *fatwā* dated December 5, 1979.

[40] Ghanem Isam, *Islamic Medical Jurisprudence*, p. 26.

not donate to heretics.[41] This is related to the value of human life under Islamic law: Muslims' lives are venerated and should be prolonged by all possible means. Those inferior to Muslims or their enemies are preserved as long as Muslims can benefit from them. For this reason Al-Shaʿrāwī objects totally to donations from living people. However, he permits donations from the dead, analogously to the Sharʿī permission to eat from a corpse in order to survive.[42]

Does an organ of the deceased defile the recipient?

Death in Islamic law is considered defiling. The question, therefore, is if an organ removed from a deceased person will render the living recipient impure; also, if an organ removed from a living donor becomes impure by being separated from the living body.

The Shāfiʿīs claim that a human being is not made impure by death. The Ḥanafīs state that a human being is made impure by death, but becomes pure again by the ablution after death. According to the Mālikīs, a dead person, even a heretic, is pure. The Ḥanbalīs conclude that a person, whether alive or dead, is pure. Almost all schools of law, then, appear to agree that the believer is pure after death, as is any organ removed from his/her body while alive.[43] No hiatus in the pure state of the Muslim recipient of an organ donation is to be feared from the transplant.

Are transplants from animals to humans allowed?

We have mentioned that during the lifetime of the Prophet, fractured bones were joined by animal bones. Historically, transplants from animals started in the 16th century. It is recorded that Muslim doctors prepared dentures from the bones of animals. Human organ donations are relatively recent, because only lately has medicine overcome the problems of rejection of another person's organ, and of preserving the organ destined for transplant. The possibility of transplanting animal parts into humans again raises the question if animal organs defile the body of the recipient.[44]

---

41 Muḥammad Abū Shādī, in: *Majallat Al-Azhar*, October 1973, p. 669.
42 *Al-Nūr*, February 22, 1989, p. 1.
43 Jād Al-Ḥaqq in the *fatwā* dated December 5, 1979.
44 Babu Sahib, Moulavi M.H., p. 129.

In this regard we found that the bone of a pure animal (*dhakiyy*) can be used for all purposes, whether it is moist or dry. Its bones are considered pure. If the animal is dead, its bone can be used only if it is dry and not moist.

There is a debate if the bones of a dog are permitted for usage, since the dog itself is held as causing impurity, although it is not included in the same list of prohibitions with swine, the blood and the carcass.[45] The Ḥanafīs even allow prayer by one in whom a bone has been replaced by a dog's bone.[46] Most schools of law allow replacement of a lost tooth with a tooth from a pure animal.[47]

Although the eating of swine's flesh (all the more its organs) is forbidden to Muslims, some scholars say that its skin, when it is the only skin available for transplant in cases of burns, may be tolerated. Others claim that in the healing process, unlike eating, there is always another option, hence pigs' skin must be avoided.[48]

May money be accepted for an organ donation?

Since the human body is not conceived as one's own property, and is viewed at most as a trust, some, like Al-Shaʿrāwī,[49] do not allow any donation whatsoever. Most scholars are more liberal, but allow no monetary compensation for the donated organs, because no *bay*ʿ (sale) can legally take place if the property is not fully owned.[50] Also, no economic need by donors can justify the injury caused by removal of their organs. Donation of organs cannot be considered a legitimate way of earning a living. There are many other ways that the Sharīʿa recommends for this.[51] Trade in organs is completely forbidden.[52] It is defined as "an inhumane act" (*ʿamal ghayr insānī*).[53]

But according to Sheikh Yaʿqūbī of Syria it is permitted to make a gift or a contribution to the donors of the organ, but it must not be of

45 Yaʿqūbī, p. 89.

46 Jād Al-Ḥaqq ʿAlī Jād Al-Ḥaqq in the *fatwā* dated December 5, 1979.

47 Ibid.

48 *Al-Liwāʾ Al-Islāmī*, February 22, 1990, p. 8.

49 In *Al-Liwāʾ Al-Islāmī*, no. 266, quoted in *Minbar Al-Islām*, June 1988.

50 Jād Al-Ḥaqq ʿAlī Jād Al-Ḥaqq in the *fatwā* dated December 5, 1979; Dr. ʿAbd Al-Fattāḥ Al-Sheikh, Rector of Al-Azhar University, in: *Al-Ahrām*, January 5, 1990, p. 15.

51 Dr. Muḥammad Sayyid Ṭanṭāwī, in: *Minbar Al-Islām*, June 1988.

52 Badar Durrez, Ahmad, p. 124; *Al-Liwāʾ Al-Islāmī*, October 31, 1991 p. 3.

53 Dr. ʿAbd Al-Munʿim Ḥasab Allah, in: *Al-Ḥaqīqa*, April 6, 1991, no. 148, p. 6.

equal value as the organ.[54] Indirectly Sheikh Yaʿqūbī admits that in practice there is a standard value for each organ...

Surprisingly, Ibn Qudāma in the 14th century allowed the sale of an organ of a living person. Based on his ruling it is allowed to reuse the organs of the deceased.[55] Since then, no one else has allowed the sale of organs.

If sale of organs were legitimized, we would probably have witnessed massive exploitation of the poor and the weak classes of society, of children and mentally disabled, etc., and also the exploitation of the third world by rich countries. At least one source claims that this is already happening in Egypt, where rich people from the Gulf pay huge sums of money for organ donations by destitute Egyptians.[56]

What is the role of the doctor?

Since organ donations are viewed as a means of saving a life that can possibly be saved, Muslim doctors are allowed to perform transplants. The doctor, whose function is to preserve the health of the body, is responsible before God and before his patients for his/her deeds.[57]

The doctor's role is not confined to the surgical stage. It is his/her task to decide that the potential organ indeed matches the recipient's body, and that the recipient has a good chance of recovery after the operation. Otherwise the operation is not justifiable. If a donation is taken from a living person, the doctor has to testify that the donor is not in any way harming his/her own life.

When several patients are waiting for the same organ, and only one such organ is available at the time, the doctor has to decide who will receive it. Indirectly, it might appear that the doctor is forced to "play God" by taking fatal decisions on who will most likely survive and who will possibly die.

It is permitted in such unfortunate circumstances for the doctors to draw lots among the relevant group of patients on the analogy of the Prophet, who decided by this means which of his wives would join him on his journeys.[58] In other cases the organ or the blood trans-

---

[54] Yaʿqūbī, p. 107.

[55] Ghanem Isam, "Islamic Medical Jurisprudence", p. 276.

[56] *Al-Liwāʾ Al-Islāmī*, October 31, 1991 p. 3.

[57] Ṭanṭāwī in *Al-Liwāʾ Al-Islāmī*, April 19, 1990, p. 8.

[58] Jād Al-Ḥaqq ʿAlī Jād Al-Ḥaqq in the *fatwā* dated December 5, 1979.

fusion must be given to the patient who might gain maximal benefit from it.[59]

The doctor's role in the process of the transplant is to mediate between the medical and the ethical-moral aspects of the transplant. Finally, the doctor also performs the surgery—the transplant and he/she is responsible to follow up the patient's recovery afterwards.

Is it permitted to establish banks for organs?

In a Muslim doctors' conference held in Spain, it was permitted that certain organs of deceased people be preserved in an organ bank, for the benefit of humanity. Muṣṭafā Al-Zarqā', a Syrian specialist in Islamic law, spoke favorably on the establishment of the eye bank.[60] Sheikh Ḥasan Ma'mūn was also in favor of an eye bank, but he rejected passing a law to authorize the removal of the eyes of all who die for the benefit of such a bank.[61] Against such a law was Dr. Ṭanṭāwī also, who nevertheless said that the eyes of dead people, whose relatives are unknown, could be removed, analogously to the permission to perform postmortems on their bodies and to use their bodies for education and criminal identification purposes.[62]

It is widely emphasized that it is the right of the deceased (before his/her death) or of his/her relatives (postmortem) to issue or not to issue permission for the removal of an organ intended for transplant.

The law seems to be more flexible when the deceased has no known relatives. One opinion states that the head of the Islamic state can decree to preserve certain vital organs of the dead in a bank, for the sake of humanity at large.[63] Still, a legal permit, of either an individual or a government, must always accompany the removal of an organ for a future transplant.

Islamic law thus provides more protection to the rights of the dead than Indian law, for example, which allows the removal of a cornea from any deceased, or than certain European countries, where unless a

---

59 Ibid.

60 Ahmad, Furqan, "Organ Transplant in Islamic Law", pp. 133-134.

61 His *fatwā* dated April 14, 1959 appeared in *Al-Fatāwā Al-Islāmiyya*, v. 7, Cairo, pp. 2552-2554.

62 *Al-Liwā' Al-Islāmī*, April 9, 1987, p. 9.

63 Ahmad, Furqan, p. 133.

person signs in advance a refusal to donate organs after his/her death, organs are automatically removed for donations according to need.[64]

Blood donations

Since the discussion about organ transplants seems always to touch upon blood donations, or it is made in analogy to blood donations, it seems worth elaborating on the latter. Blood donations are the most common of all and the simplest to perform from a medical point of view. Since blood is donated only by living donors, who agree to the donation, it can serve as a model for donations made in the lifetime of the donor.

Although blood, when separated from the body, is considered impure, it may be transferred from the healthy to the sick, when a qualified doctor affirms that this might cure the sick person and when the donor's health is not endangered.[65] Saving one's life is an *ʿamal ṣāliḥ* (righteous deed), and if a blood donation saves life, the donation is legitimate.[66]

The blood transfusion does not make the recipient impure because it is in the form of an injection, not via the mouth, nor is it to be viewed as *damm masfūḥ* (spilled blood);[67] the latter is often considered impure.

On the other hand, whoever donates blood (like the donor of milk) is rewarded in the Hereafter.[68] Al-Shaʿrāwī even allows a monetary compensation for blood donations, although it is recommended to donate blood for no compensation: the donor's reward in the Hereafter is doubled that way.[69] Those who support the sale of blood compare it to the hiring of a wetnurse, which is legitimized by Qur'an 2,233. Those

---

64 Siddiqi, "Legal Issues in Human-Organ Transplant: Indian Perspective", p. 154.

65 Ḥasanayn Muḥammad Makhlūf, "jawāz naql al-damm lilʿilāj", in: *Fatāwā Sharʿiyya wa Buḥūth Islāmiyya*, 3rd edition, Cairo 1971, v. 2, p. 218; Sheikh Ḥasan Ma'mūn in a *fatwā* dated June 9, 1954, which was published in *Al-Fatāwā Al-Islāmiyya*, v. 7, 1982, p. 2495.

66 Al-Shaʿrāwī, *Al-Fatāwā, kull mā yuhimm Al-Muslim fī ḥayātihi wayawmihi waghaddihi*, Cairo 1981, v. 1, p. 31; *Al-Muslimūn*, July 5, 1991, p. 8 (The Fatwā Committee at Al-Azhar).

67 ʿAbd Al-Ḥamīd Al-Sayyid Shāhīn, in: *Majallat Al-Azhar*, June 1987, p. 1390.

68 ʿAbd Allah Al-Mushidd, "mā ra'y al-dīn fī al-tabarruʿ bil-damm", in: *Al-Ahrām*, July 26, 1985, p. 15.

69 Al-Shaʿrāwī, "al-tabarruʿ bildamm", in: *Al-Fatāwā*, Cairo, n.d., v. 7, pp. 63-64.

who object to the sale of blood claim that it is a part of the body, which is owned by Allah alone, not by any human being.[70]

Muslims are often concerned if blood donations from a man to a woman, and vice versa, may establish a relationship between the two that may prevent a later marriage option between them. Likewise, they wonder if the anonymity of donors maintained by the blood banks is not an impediment to marriage contracts.

To refute such fears it is decisively stated that blood, unlike milk, is not a barrier to marriage. In addition, it is emphasized that milk too establishes a semi-brotherhood relation only during the first two years of a baby's life, when milk constitutes the entire nutrition.[71]

Blood donations of a non-Muslim to a Muslim are permitted if the patient's health depends on it.[72] We did not discover if the opposite case, i.e. a Muslim's donation to a non-Muslim, is allowed as well.

If an analogy between blood donations and organ transplant is made, it seems that there should be no objection to donations by males to females, and vice versa. Also, the donations of a single donor to both a man and a woman should not hinder the future marriage of the latter two, although such a case precisely was not covered in our sources.

Summary

Islamic law permits all organ transplants, although it speaks more often of transplants that statistically occur most: blood, cornea and skin donations.

Most of the dilemmas which theologists treat are related to the donors: Who should they be? Is their dignity endangered? When exactly does death occur? Who is to decide about the donation when the donor has already died? etc. Not much thought is given to the process of transplant itself and to its medical aspects, but this is understood considering the nature of the discussion and discussants.

---

70 *Al-Liwā' Al-Islāmī*, July 11, 1991 (*muftī* 'Abd Al-Munṣif Maḥmūd); *Al-Muslimūn*, July 5, 1991 (The Fatwā Committee at al-Azhar).

71 Sheikh 'Aṭiyya Ṣaqr, "hal yuḥarrim naql al-damm al-zawāj, kal-riḍā'?", in: *Al-Ahrām*, January 28, 1983, p. 13; *Liwā' Al-Islām*, October 1951, p. 318; *Al-Islām Waṭan*, December 1987, no. 8, p. 50; *Fatāwā Islāmiyya*, 1st edition, Beirut 1988, v. 2, p. 342.

72 Sheikh 'Abd Allah Al-Mushidd, in: *Al-Ahrām*, July 1, 1982, p. 12.

Questions such as: How long after death should a transplant take place? What happens to the organ if it is rejected by the recipient's body? What should be done with the organ when the recipient dies during the transplant operation? How many recurring transplants should be performed to save one patient? etc., have not been discussed by the jurists of Islam so far.

Only several issues among those enumerated above are what we might call "typically Islamic." They include the dilemma if an organ from a dead person or from an animal defiles the Muslim recipient; the perception of purity in Islamic law influences Islamic lifestyle and social norms immensely. Also, the preference for donors whom Islamic law grades as second-rate citizens, and the acceptance of "ordinary Muslims" only as the last resort, derives from the infavorable Islamic view of the foreigner, the non-Muslim and the criminal.

Issues related to the sanctity of the human body, semi-ownership of it, accepting payment for donation, the role of the doctor, etc., can be of concern to other monotheists as well.

CHAPTER FIVE

COSMETIC AND SEX CHANGE SURGERIES

Cosmetic surgery and sex change surgery, different as they may appear to be, have at least one common feature, namely, they both involve the introduction of physical changes into the body. Both express dissatisfaction with the body as it is. The motive for cosmetic surgeries is usually the desire to improve one's appearance, regardless of whether this appearance is hereditary or the result of some accident or misfortune. The motive for sex change surgery is either that the person carries both male and female sexual organs and wishes to remove those of one sex so as to become identified completely as a member of the other; or the person may be unable psychologically and mentally to identify with his/her sex and wishes to become a member of the other.

Both cosmetic and sex change surgeries are apt to evoke the theological dilemma of whether human beings, with or without the interference of surgeons, are permitted to make any changes in the human body, which is after all *khalq Allah* (a creation of God), and which is not fully owned by any human being, as has already been explained in our discussion of transplants.

Cosmetic surgery

Contemporary *muftīs* are often not ignorant of the psychological problems which an unusual or unpleasant appearance might cause. When cosmetic surgery is permitted by them, it is often justified as a means to solve such problems. In this regard, it is often recalled that one Companion of the Prophet, named ʿArfaja, lost his nose in battle, and he replaced it with a silver nose. When his nose started to stink, obviously causing the Companion much embarrassment, the Prophet ordered him to replace it with a golden nose. By analogy, Muslims are permitted to get rid of distorted features in their face or body, as long as "the creation of God" remains in its original form.[1] This requirement that the "creation of God" remains unaltered is not further ex-

[1] *Al-Liwāʾ Al-Islāmī*, January 18, 1990 p. 7.

plained by any legal source. The result is that the interpretation of a certain surgery as causing/not causing *taghyīr khalq Allah* (changing the creation of God) remains flexible.

For example, several *fatāwā* were in favour of surgically removing the sixth finger in a hand or the sixth toe in a foot, so that the child would not be mocked by his friends. Permission was granted on the grounds of avoiding embarrassment, pain,[2] and even as a means of augmenting beauty, since it was claimed that God appreciates beauty.[3]

Surgery for straightening crooked teeth for beauty purposes was allowed to a woman, if the defect caused people to avoid her and consequently jeopardised her chances of marrying. This surgery was not considered a *taghyīr khalq Allah*, and it was emphasized again that God appreciates beauty.[4] The use of teeth made of gold and platinum was permitted when necessary, in recognition that the use of other metals could be harmful.[5] This permission must also be evaluated against the abhorrence in Islamic law of the use of precious metals, especially gold and especially by men.[6] In other words, the dislike for gold is superseded by the desire to solve the dental and orthodontic problems of Muslims.

As for nose reconstructions, despite the model set by the Prophet's Companion ʿArfaja, as mentioned above, Al-Shaʿrāwī pronounces a completely negative approach. When a woman asked him if changing her hooked nose was permissible, he paid no attention to her misery at all. Instead, he embarked on a lengthy discourse meant to prove that beauty must never be measured in human terms. God created both beauty and ugliness, and the physically handicapped and crippled were often compensated in a different area or talent (see for example the achievements of the deaf Beethoven and the blind *Ṭaha Ḥusayn*). Al-Shaʿrāwī actually conveys that ugliness is not so bad after all. Finally he charges the Greeks with responsibility for formulating the

---

[2] Muftī Aḥmad Haraydī, in: *Al-Fatāwā Al-Islāmiyya*, v. 7, pp. 2569-2570 (the *fatwā* was dated May 22, 1968); Muftī ʿAṭiyya Ṣaqr, in: *Māyū*, December 2, 1985, p. 11.

[3] *Al-Liwāʾ Al-Islāmī*, April 16, 1987, p. 6. See the tradition attributed to the Prophet on this issue in *Sunan Al-Tirmidhī*, Medina 1964, v. 3, p. 244.

[4] *Al-Umma Al-Islāmiyya*, November 1985, p. 7.

[5] *Majallat Al-Tawḥīd* Jumādā Al-Ākhira, 1410, p. 10.

[6] Men are forbidden to use gold jewelry and women are not, on the basis of a tradition attributed to the Prophet. A silver ring, if it does not exceed a certain weight, is permitted. See: Dr. Wahba Al-Zuḥaylī, *Al-Fiqh Al-Islāmī waAdillatuhu*, 3rd edition, Damascus 1989, v. 3, pp. 547-548.

standards of beauty, but states that they were unable to create even a statue according to these standards. No one knows what the ingredients of beauty are, he concludes, and it might well be that a hooked nose is one of them.[7]

Al-Shaʿrāwī is exceptional among the *muftī*s in that he adheres to his opinion and ignores the feelings and distress of the inquiring woman. In a sense he remains in the realm of dogmatics and refuses to lean towards a consideration of the particular case presented to him and its unique features. His reluctance to approve a certain *taghyīr khalq Allah* is very stubborn, and unmatched by most of the *muftī*s who discussed the subject.

By contrast, *muftī* ʿAbd Al-Munṣif Maḥmūd permitted nose surgery on a woman whose natural nose caused her much distress. He did not view the surgery as "*taghyīr khalq Allah*". Maḥmūd too relied on the tradition mentioned by Al-Tirmidhī about the Prophet's Companion who lost his nose in battle.[8]

A man who inquired if it was permissible to uplift drooping eyelids received a positive answer, based on the realization of the *muftī* that although the surgery was cosmetic, the drooping eyelids were nevertheless a source of inconvenience.[9]

The lifting of a woman's eyebrows is generally forbidden by the Sharīʿa, as is the use of powders and creams, on the assumption that these are intended to change what God has created. However, if the cause is medical, a married woman needs her husband's permission for such intervention; a single woman should undergo it only for hygienic reasons, not in order to deceive her prospective groom. Lifting the eyebrows merely for cosmetic purposes is completely forbidden, because the woman must not beautify herself for the public eye, according to the Ḥanbalīs.[10] In fact, all schools of law state that a woman's beauty must be kept indoors, and it is only for her husband to enjoy.

Plucking out excessive hair from a woman's eyebrows is often considered "changing the creation of God", and therefore is forbidden.[11] Even hair growing on a woman's cheeks or forehead is to be

---

[7] Al-Shaʿrāwī, *Miʾat Suʾāl waJawāb*, Cairo n.d., pp. 14-16.

[8] "tajmīl al-anf al-mushawwah", in: *Al-Liwāʾ Al-Islāmī*, August 1, 1991, p. 6.

[9] *Majallat Al-Tawḥīd*, Shawāl 1410, p. 28 (*muftī* Muḥammad ʿAlī ʿAbd Al-Raḥīm).

[10] *Al-Liwāʾ Al-Islāmī*, January 4, 1990 (*muftī* Dr. ʿAbd Al-Salām Al-Sukkarī).

[11] Al-Shaʿrāwī, *Al-Fatāwā*, Cairo n.d., v. 3, p. 32; *Al-Fatāwā Al-Islāmiyya*, 1st edition, Beirut 1988, v. 3, pp. 200-201 (a *fatwā* by Ibn Bāz).

left untouched. The prohibition is always founded in the tradition that "God will curse those who make tattoos and those who pluck out hair."[12]

One *fatwā* excepted from among those mentioned in that tradition women on whose faces a beard or a moustache happened to grow.[13] They were excluded probably because a beard or a moustache rendered their appearance similar to that of men. This might cause confusion in differentiating between the sexes, which is intolerable in Islamic law. It is preferable, therefore, for such women to remove the male features from their faces.

Apparently, anything considered a cosmetic technique and not a medical necessity is forbidden. It is explained in one place that the eyebrows were intended to absorb sweat and block it from flowing into the eyes,[14] so to remove the eyebrows wholly or partly is to disregard God's wisdom in placing the eyebrows where they are. Only one source saw no harm in plucking facial hair, explaining that this was not meant "to change the creation of God".[15] The removal of body hair on a woman, however, is not objected to,[16] either because her body may be seen only by her husband or because body hair seems to disturb the notion of purity of the woman's body and its readiness for sexual contact.

The *muftīs* generally show sensitivity to the embarrassment and psychological difficulties caused by certain appearances, and some *muftīs* permit certain major surgical procedures, even transplants, which decidedly "change the creation of God" still more. Yet plucking thick eyebrows unexpectedly elicits strong opposition. Moreover, no concern for the psychological problems that an excess of facial hair can cause a woman is evident in our sources. Nor did we find any attention paid to the possibility that some hirsute women may never be requested in marriage, so their hairiness may become a cause of their social isolation, something which technically can easily be corrected.

Dieting to lose weight, if intended to beautify and improve one's appearance, is objected to. But if the same dieting can be proved

---

12 *Sunan Al-Tirmidhī*, v. 5, p. 193.

13 *Al-Nūr*, August 5, 1990, p. 7.

14 *Majallat Al-Tawḥīd*, Jumādā Al-Ūlā 1410, p. 19; *Al-Daʿwa*, March 14, 1991 (*muftī* ʿAbd Al-ʿAzīz b. ʿAbd Allah b. Bāz).

15 *Al-Nūr*, August 5, 1990, p. 7.

16 *Al-Jumʿa*, September-October 1989, p. 21 (*muftī* Sheikh ʿAbd Allah Abū ʿĪd).

beneficial to health and does not seem to harm the body it is permissible.[17]

A bald woman may wear a wig even thought the use of wigs is forbidden by Islamic law. It is emphasized that there is a difference between beautifying and the removal of defects. Whatever cannot be classified as removing a defect is necessarily classified as "beautifying", hence forbidden. Therefore, the attachment of a golden nose to a man's face was permitted, since he had lost his nose in battle. But nose surgery, and the removal of a black mole, are forbidden, if intended only for cosmetic purposes.[18] Changes in the eyebrows are all viewed as changing God's creation, not even as beautifying, hence strictly forbidden.[19]

Sex change surgery

Surgery to change sex is legitimized in both directions provided certain conditions stipulated by law are fulfilled: (a) concealed female organs are found in a man and concealed male organs are found in a woman; (b) an experienced physician attests to the existence of such organs, and predicts that after their exposure the person will be able to conduct a fulfilled life in both the physical and the moral senses. A mere desire to change sex, with the absence of these prerequisites, does not justify sex-change surgery.[20] This is based on the fiqh attitude to the *mukhannath* or *khanthā* (androgynous).[21]

A recently published case of sex change is that of the medical student Sayyid ʿAbd Allah, who sensed the existence of female organs in his body, and this led Dr. ʿIzzat ʿAshm Allah of the Umbāba Hospital to remove the student's penis and cut in his body an opening similar to a vagina. The student then changed his name to Sally.

---

[17] *Al-Jumhūriyya*, June 1, 1983, p. 5 (Sheikh Ibrāhīm Jalhūm).

[18] *Al-Fatāwā Al-Islāmiyya*, 1st edition, Beirut 1988, v.3, pp. 201-202 (a *fatwā* by Ibn ʿAthimīn).

[19] Ibid., p. 200.

[20] Jād Al-Ḥaqq ʿAlī Jād Al-Ḥaqq, in: *Al-Ahrām* January 23, 1981, p. 9, and in: *Al-Fatāwā Al-Islāmiyya*, v. 10, pp. 3501-3503 (the *fatwā* is dated June 27, 1981).

[21] According to Ibn ʿAbbās, a *mukhannath* is a man who has no erection. Mujāhid and Qatāda claimed that a *mukhannath* is a man without sexual desire for women. Shāfiʿīs claimed that a *mukhannath* is a feminine man (soft speech, sinuous walk, etc.), but must be treated legally as a man: for instance, he cannot be invited into a woman's residence lest he describe her to others. See: Dr. Wahba Al-Zuḥaylī, *Al-Fiqh Al-Islāmī waAdillatuhu*, v. 7, pp. 19-21.

Muftī ʿAṭiyya Ṣaqr explained that this surgery was unjustified by Islamic law and that the student himself was a sinner. His reasoning was that an inclination toward the other sex must not necessarily entail a change of sex. In the surgery on the student Sayyid ʿAbd Allah, the penis was removed but no female organs were revealed in its stead. the student thus became neither a male nor a female. Moreover, his feminine inclination could not be satisfied by any legitimate sexual contact.[22]

In other words, since the student's male organ was removed for the sake of non-existent female parts, Sheikh ʿAṭiyya Ṣaqr viewed the student as a *mukhannath* following the surgery, not before it, when the student probably felt like a *mukhannath* although legally he was not. According to the *muftī* this surgery solved nothing, but instead created a problem. Therefore the surgery was considered unnecessary and illegitimate.

The principle which seems to emerge from both cosmetic and sex surgery is that when a procedure, even though definitely causing a change in creation, seems to solve a person's stressful emotional situation, it wins the *muftī*s' approval. Sex changes too can be justified by Islamic law if they seem able to help a person classify himself/herself as either a man or a woman. This openness must be emphasized against the fixed biological and social roles which Islamic law and theology clearly allocated to men and women, roles which are considered God's decree. Needless to say, when medically required all surgery is justified. Cosmetic purposes, if not convincingly linked to health implications, are doomed to be disallowed as legitimizing any surgery.

---

22 *Minbar Al-Islām*, October 1988, pp. 132-134.

CHAPTER SIX

MEDICAL ASPECTS OF ISLAMIC WORSHIP

Islamic worship, as embodied in the five pillars of Islam, often requires a certain physical competence, in addition to the spiritual devotion naturally expected of a believer. Prayers, which take place five times a day, include prostrations, kneelings, prolonged standing and other less strenuous movements. The Fast of Ramadan each year is a month-long abstinence during the daylight hours from eating, drinking and consequently from the intake of most medicines. The pilgrimage to Mecca (*ḥajj*) often entails a long journey from and back to the pilgrim's residence, in addition to about a week of consecutive rituals which take place inside and outside the city of Mecca. All these rituals require some physical effort, the degree of which obviously varies from one person to another. For the elderly and infirm among the pilgrims the experience of the *ḥajj* can become almost intolerable.

Testimony (*Shahāda*) and almsgiving (*zakāt*) are the two pillars among the five that do not appear to require physical fitness; We will not discuss them, therefore, in this chapter.

Islamic law, based on the Qur'an, realized as early as the Middle Ages the physical difficulties which the pillars of prayer, fast and pilgrimage may sometimes pose, and offered concessions to certain groups of people, such as the sick, the pregnant and breast-feeding mother, and the handicapped (as well as for the traveller and the soldier in combat), who are not able to fulfil these duties to the letter.

Some of the concessions in the service are that when the situation so requires a prayer can be shortened, or two prayers can be joined to save time, or the physical movements can be modified and made easier—all according to the circumstances in which the praying Muslim happens to be.[1]

As for Ramadan, if for some reason a Muslim is physically unable to fast, he might substitute the missed days of fast by giving the poor a

---

[1] Most legal books include a special chapter concerning the concessions during prayer for the sick, often titled *ṣalāt al-marīḍ* (the prayer of the sick). See for example: Al-Sarakhsī, *Al-Mabsūṭ*, Beirut 1978, v.1, pp. 212-218.

certain amount of food against each missed day, or by donating charity for each missed day, or by fasting for the given number of missed days at a time after Ramadan; the last option is available to one whose physical disability prevented fasting in the first place, was temporary and has in the meantime improved.[2]

Verse 3,97 one of the two Qur'anic verses (2,196: 3,97) which establish the duty of the *ḥajj*, also stipulates that only the "owner" of *istiṭā'a* (ability) is required to perform the duty. Commentators often interpret "ability" to include, among several factors, good health.[3] In other words, a sick person (like a very poor person) is held to be lacking in the "ability", hence he/she is exempt from fulfilling the duty unless his/her health improves.

Considering that the *ḥajj* is only a once-in-a-lifetime obligation, incumbent upon those who *own* the "ability," the sick who do not have such an "ability," are actually allowed in Islamic law never to perform the duty, unless they are wealthy and can afford to hire another person to perform the *ḥajj* in their stead. If they are sick and poor, they are not even asked to compensate for the unfulfilled *ḥajj* in any form of charity or otherwise.

The flexibility shown by Islamic law toward the physically disabled is apparently not abused by devout Muslims. Rather the contrary is evinced from contemporary *fatāwā*; devout Muslims prefer to perform the duties to the best of their ability and not to evade performance by means of the legitimate concessions.

The quantitative aspect in contemporary *fatāwā* also indicates that the fulfilment of prayer, fast and *ḥajj* is still extremely important to the modern Muslim. The numerous questions on these topics which are addressed to the *muftis* are indeed often repetitive. The essence of all questions, whether they refer to prayer, fast or *ḥajj* is if the performance of the religious duty while handicapped, or aided by medi-

---

[2] The legal literature differentiates between *qaḍā'*—a compensation for swallowing a non-nourishing object or a medicine, and *kafāra*—a compensation for swallowing a nourishing object, which involves sin (*jināya*). Sometimes a combination of the two is required, if, for example, a person swallowed two objects, each belonging to one of the two types as described above. *Qaḍā'* is simply the completion of the full number of fasting days after Ramadan, assuming that one violated the fast for a legitimate Shar'ī reason. If he violated the fast for another reason, *kafāra* in the form of charity must accompany *qaḍā'*. If a person cannot fast at all times, *kafāra* is the only step required of him/her. See for example: Al-Sarakhsī, *Al-Mabsūṭ*, v. 3, pp. 136-138.

[3] Al-Ghazzālī, *Iḥyā' 'Ulūm Al-Dīn*, Cairo 1957, v. 1, p. 246; Ibn Kathīr, *Tafsir Al-Qur'ān Al-'Aẓīm*, Cairo n.d., v. 1, p. 386.

cations and medical instruments, renders the performance of the duty invalid or not.

Since a very basic requirement for the valid performance of prayer, fast and *ḥajj* is an appropriate state of physical purity, most questions center on the physical flaws or/and treatments that may violate the state of purity and those that do not.

The relevant chapters in Islamic law concerning *ṭahāra* (purity) are very detailed and comprehensive, to the point that one may wonder at the large number of questions that still address the same "old" issues. At the same time, however, the *mufti*s are also approached to rule on new medications and medical devices which the modern man and woman have learnt to use and which have made their lives more tolerable. Infirm Muslims hope that these devices will be approved by the *mufti*s and not found to conflict with religious worship. But the questions themselves leave room for the opposite verdict as well. Because of the differences in their occurrence and in the various physical requirements of prayer, fast and *ḥajj*, each deserves a separate discussion.

Prayer

Most of the questions concerning the prayer actually focus on the state of purity which must precede prayer and be maintained throughout its performance, which takes place at least five times daily.

One person inquired how to perform the small ablution (*wuḍū'*) without having arms. He was advised that if the amputation was above the elbow, no *wuḍū'* was necessary. But, if the elbow existed the stump had to be washed.[4]

A woman whose leg was in cast was advised to wash before prayer every part of her body except for the part in cast. That part had to be purified by sand (*tayammum*) so that water would not reach the broken leg.[5] *Tayammum* was recommended also for a person suffering from rheumatism, and for whom the use of cold, or even hot water could be harmful. The final decision was left to the discretion of the patient himself or a trustworthy doctor.[6]

---

[4] *Minbar Al-Islām*, May 1990, p. 50 (a *fatwā* issued by 'Aṭiyya Ṣaqr).

[5] Dr. Ḥusaynī Abū Farḥa, in: *Al-Ahrām*, August 19, 1983, p. 13: "kayfa ataṭahhar wasāqī fī al-jibs."

[6] Muftī Badr Al-Mutawallī 'Abd Al-Bāsiṭ, in: *Liwā' Al-Islām*, August 1971, no. 10, pp. 54-55.

Several questions deal with the problem of loss of control over the bladder during prayer, and after ablution had already taken place. The problem of course is that those suffering from constant discharge of urine are never completely pure for prayer purposes. *Muftīs* usually excuse these patients and advise them to perform an ablution, place a clean piece of cloth where their clothes usually become stained, then pray. Whatever escapes their body afterwards is not considered their fault, and their prayer remains valid.[7]

In the same line of thought, a woman who continued to bleed after her period had definitely ended was advised to perform *ghusl* (large ablution), to mark thus the end of her period, then to perform *wuḍū'* before every prayer and then pray. The continuous bleeding was perceived to be beyond her control or explanation. She was incidentally also advised to seek medical treatment.[8]

In another *fatwā*, the "sticky matter" that escapes the body after urination was considered invalidating the *wuḍū'*, but not invalidating the *ghusl* which precedes Friday and holiday public prayer.[9] This might be seen as a concession toward the believer who has made an effort to attend a prayer in the mosque and who possibly arrived from a long distance.

A sick person who suffered from flatulence with foul smells emanating constantly from his body complained that his problem was uncontrollable, and as soon as he performed one ablution the bad odors forced him to perform another, so that he missed the time of prayer. He was advised to perform only one ablution before each prayer, and as soon as the prayer time had passed to perform the ablution in readiness for the next prayer.[10]

Islamic legal literature has since medieval times taken care of people who could not stand up, bend or prostrate themselves during prayer, and they were permitted to pray sitting or even lying down. Most contemporary questions deal more with gynecological and urological ailments which are believed to be curable by medications. Those that cannot be solved in this way are the exception. Even patients who suffer from incurable diseases insist on praying, and the

---

[7] Ibrāhīm Al-Waqfī wa'Abd Al-Munṣif Maḥmūd, in: *Al-Liwā' Al-Islāmī*, February 22, 1990, p. 7.

[8] Muḥammad 'Abd Allah Al-Khaṭīb, in: *Al-Nūr*, August 30, 1989, p. 8.

[9] Muḥammad 'Alī 'Abd Al-Raḥīm, in: *Majallat Al-Tawḥīd*, no. 5, Jumādā Al-Ūlā 1408, p. 24.

[10] *Al-Nūr*, August 7, 1991, p. 7.

muftīs, in an attempt to demonstrate the ease of religion (*yusr*), not its strictness (*'usr*), usually side with the devout patients while overlooking their "spoiled" ablutions.

Ḥajj

With regard to the pilgrimage we found that people worry that the use of an artificial leg or a device attached to the leg, intended to facilitate walking, might render their *ḥajj* invalid. The *muftīs* often sympathize with the person in pain. People who have difficulty walking barefoot, for example, are permitted to use an artificial device. They are also encouraged to use cork sandals. As long as the heel is exposed no compensation for this concession is due. However, a rubber shoe covering the heel is equated with clothes with seams, which are forbidden during the *ḥajj*. The wearing of such a shoe requires compensation for the "defective" *ḥajj* by slaughtering a lamb or feeding six poor people, or fasting three days.

By analogy, a sick person may use a hernia belt (*ḥizām fatq*) while wrapped in the *iḥrām* (a special white seamless cloth used during the *ḥajj*) or while performing *sa'y* (running between *Ṣafā* and *Marwa*) or *ṭawāf* (circumambulation of the Ka'ba), even when there is a seam in the belt.[11]

In other words, as long as the "relief" provided by the artificial limb, the shoe or the hernia belt does not violate the basic requirements that the heels remain at all times exposed, or alternately that the *iḥrām* is seamless, the patient is able to continue a valid *ḥajj*.[12]

Since a state of purity is essential for the performance of the *ḥajj* as well, a woman may postpone her menstrual period by the use of injections, lest her period invalidate her *ḥajj*. This is so even though among the *ḥajj* rituals, only the *ṭawāf*, like prayer, requires such purity, which menstrual bleeding nullifies. If the woman vomits, even during the *ṭawāf*, she may continue the ritual. Vomiting does not invalidate the *wuḍū'* unless it is brought on deliberately. She is advised, however, to carry with her a nylon bag to avoid staining others.[13]

---

[11] *Al-Liwā' Al-Islāmī*, June 13, 1991, p. 17 (a *fatwā* by Dr. 'Abd Al-Mun'im Tu'aylab from King 'Abd Al-'Azīz University of Jedda).

[12] *Al-Nūr*, May 29, 1991, p. 7 (based on a *fatwā* by Sheikh Muḥammad Khāṭir, in: *Al-Fatāwā Al-Islāmiyya*, v. 5, no. 1833); *Al-Liwā' Al-Islāmī*, May 3, 1990 (a *fatwā* by Muḥammad Sayyid Ṭanṭāwī).

[13] *Al-Liwā' Al-Islāmī*, June 13, 1991, p. 17.

Nowadays, with means of transportation more comfortable and affordable, women have a better chance of performing the *ḥajj* than before. They resort to the new medical devices such as the contraceptive pill and specific injections to delay menstruation, and thus circumvent the natural barriers which in the past interfered with women's ability to fulfil the duty of the *ḥajj* as they might have planned and wished.

The *muftīs*, again, seem to overlook the possible interference with the natural physiology of women, which theologically is God's plan, in favor of legitimizing medical means of evading the "obstacles" created by this same physiology—at least temporarily.

In the foregoing examples, special consideration was given to medical conditions that are uniquely female: menstruation and pregnancy. Both a recognition of the special problems of women and a desire to facilitate their participation in the *ḥajj* emerge from these examples.

Fast of Ramadan

The fast of Ramadan, which is compulsory for every healthy adult, male or female, is held as a very important commandment, to the degree that Muslims who usually do not observe the religious code of behavior would still attempt to fulfil the duty of the fast. The Qur'an itself defines the concessions to those who for legitimate reasons cannot endure part of the fast or the all of it. Qur'an 2, 184-185 reads "(Fast) a certain number of days; and (for) him who is sick among you, or on a journey, (the same) number of other days; and for those who can afford it there is a ransom: the feeding of a man in need—But whoso doeth good of his own accord, it is better for him: and that ye fast is better for you if ye did but know—the month of Ramadan in which was revealed the Qur'an, a guidance for mankind, and clear proofs of the guidance, and the Criterion (of right and wrong). And whosoever of you is present, let him fast the month and whosoever of you is sick or on a journey, (let him fast the same) number of other days. Allah desireth for you ease; He desireth not hardship for you; and (He desireth) that ye should complete the period, ..."[14]

[14] Translated according to M.M. Pickthall, *The Meaning of the Glorious Koran*, USA n.d.

As indicated in the Qur'an, these concessions are not exclusively health-related, but the health condition is given deep consideration among them.[15]

The concessions are usually in the form of charity in a certain stated sum or a number of meals to be distributed among the poor. Alternative fasting days, to substitute for the days of Ramadan not fasted, are another option, but this applies only to those who have fully recovered from their earlier illness.

Despite the wide range of concessions, the *fatāwā* hold much evidence that sick people wish to fast, even while supported by various medical aids, as long as their fast is deemed valid.

A person suffering from a heart problem, whom his physicians have recommended not to fast, is encouraged to obey them and to fast again only after he has recovered, or to give two meals to one poor person (*miskīn*) for each day of the fast he misses.[16]

Similar advice was given to a person suffering from kidney failure who must take in large quantities of liquids. He was advised to follow the Muslim doctor's instructions and not let the fast worsen his illness. He too was instructed to feed one *miskīn* for each day of fast missed.[17]

A diabetic patient was given the same answer too. It was explained in his case that the *kafāra* (compensation) due was a *madd min qamḥ* (half a cup of flour) for a poor person per each day of fast not fasted.[18]

A person suffering from ulcers who must eat a small amount of food every two hours was advised not to fast at all, and instead to feed a poor person for each day he did not fast. This method suffices for as long as he is ill, but after recovery he is urged to fast the number of days he missed, as far as he is able.[19]

Sick people often inquire whether medications that they have to consume on a regular basis violate the fast, or not. These people are concerned that owing to their continuous illness they might never be

---

[15] Old Age, for this matter, can sometimes become a difficult health condition, and the aged person then is exempt from fasting and is required to feed one *miskīn* (poor person) for each day not fasted. See: *Al-Liwā' Al-Islāmī*, March 29, 1990, p. 17.

[16] *Al-Muslimūn*, April 5, 1991, p. 8. The *fatwā* was issued by the Fatwā Committee at Al-Azhar.

[17] *Al-Nūr*, May 3, 1989, p. 8 (a *fatwā* by 'Abd Al-Fattāḥ 'Āshūr, a professor at Al-Azhar).

[18] *Al-Nūr*, July 5, 1989, p. 8 (a *fatwā* by the previous *muftī*).

[19] *Al-Liwā' Al-Islāmī*, March 22, 1990, p. 8 (a *fatwā* by *muftī* Ibrāhīm Al-Waqfī).

able to fast properly again, since the intake of the medications violates the fast; yet only through medication can they live an almost normal life, including the fulfilment of religious duties. The paradox is that *with* most of the medications the fast is invalid, but *without* them it is impossible, and even a health hazard.

The *muftīs* are thus approached to mediate between religious tenets and the intake of certain medications. For example, they are often asked if the use of nose drops and eye drops invalidates the fast.

Eye drops are not usually considered as invalidating the fast, since according to the Ḥanafīs and Shāfiʿis the eye is not a *manfadh* (hole, opening) through which liquids enter the stomach.[20] As opposed to this, Dr. Ṭanṭāwī has decreed that the use of eye drops is "undesired" (*makrūh*), even if they do not reach the stomach. If they do their intake is definitely forbidden. It is safest, therefore, to use eye drops after the fasting hours are over.[21]

Nose drops, are usually held to violate the fast, because they eventually reach the stomach. A woman suffering from nasal congestion which disturbs her breathing, as a result of *ḥasāsiyyat al-damm* (allergy), and she cannot respire properly without the use of nasal drops, unless a *rabw ṣadrī* (asthma) develops, was advised to stop fasting immediately, use the drops and compensate for the breached fast via feeding a *miskīn*, as described above.[22]

Another person, who used a *jihāz bikhākha* (inhalator) to treat the *rabw* disease, asked if this violated his fast. The response was that if the medication travels through the instrument into his stomach, via the nose or the mouth, his fast is invalidated. But if the medication does not enter his stomach the fast remains valid.

In case the fast was violated, once the patient recovers from the disease he should complete the number of fasting days missed or violated. But if the illness is incurable the patient must not fast at all, but instead feed a *miskīn* for every day not fasted.[23]

The rule with regard to injections is like that of the medications: if the material reaches the stomach it violates the fast even if it was in-

---

[20] *Al-Ahrām*, June 24, 1984, p. 12 (the *muftī* was ʿAbd Al-Laṭīf Ḥamza); *Al-Ahrām*, July 1, 1982, p. 13.

[21] *Al-Umma Al-Islāmiyya*, March 1991, p. 6.

[22] *Al-Liwāʾ Al-Islāmī*, March 29, 1990, p. 8; *Al-Muslimūn*, March 22, 1991, p. 8 (a *fatwā* by Muḥammad Sayyid Ṭanṭāwī).

[23] *Al-Liwāʾ Al-Islāmī*, March 22, 1990, p. 8 (a *fatwā* by Sheikh Ibrāhīm Al-Waqfī).

jected into the thigh, the buttocks or the arm.[24] Maḥmūd Shaltūt, however, stated that no injections violate the fast, because whether subcutaneous or intravenous they never enter the place of food and drink, and a fasting person is therefore permitted to receive them.[25]

The division between injections that violate the fast and those that do not seems to depend on whether their material reaches the digestive system or not.[26] Even vitamin and glucose injections, if not believed to reach the stomach, are permitted to the fasting person, although they may well be for nourishment and recuperation.[27]

The debate about enema (*ḥuqna sharjiyya*) also centers on whether it reaches the stomach, thereby invalidating the fast, as most jurists claim,[28] or if it does *not* violate the fast, as according to the Mālikīs, because it does not reach the stomach.[29]

Tranquilizing injections are permitted during the Ramadan fasting, if they are intended to protect the body against harm. Even stimulating injections do not invalidate the fast, if the circumstances at one's workplace so require.[30]

A related question is whether immunization measures against illnesses such as cholera, smallpox, typhus, etc., if taken during Ramadan, violate the fast. The same rule as above, in accordance with Ḥanafī and Shāfiʿī teachings, is applied here too; as long as the serum does not enter the stomach or the brain via the "openings" which are primarily for feeding purposes—the mouth and the nose—the fast remains valid.[31]

As for vomit, which is usually expelled through the mouth, and therefore could cause violation of the fast, most legal scholars rely on the Prophet's conclusion that if the vomiting was deliberate it violates

---

[24] Ibid.

[25] *Al-Liwā' Al-Islāmī*, March 29, 1990, p. 7. A similar opinion was also expressed by Al-Sayyid Al-Ṣāwī, in: *Manār Al-Islām*, March 1991, p. 80.

[26] *Al-Muslimūn*, March 29, 1991, p. 8 (the *muftī* was ʿAbd Allah b. Sulaymān b. Manīʿ).

[27] *Al-Ahrām*, June 12, 1984, p. 12 (a *fatwā* by ʿAbd Al-Laṭīf Ḥamza).

[28] *Manār Al-Islām*, March 1991, p. 80.

[29] *Al-Liwā' Al-Islāmī*, April 12, 1990, p. 6 (a *fatwā* by ʿAbd Al-Munṣif Maḥmūd).

[30] *Al-Muslimūn*, July 12, 1991, p. 8 (issued by the Fatwā Committee in Saudi Arabia).

[31] *Al-Liwā' Al-Islāmī*, March 22, 1990, p. 8; *Al-Nūr*, March 27, 1991, p. 7 (a *fatwā* by ʿAbd Al-Majīd Salīm).

the fast. If it was unintentional the fast remains valid.[32] Even blood flowing from the gums, if not swallowed, and cleared from the mouth, does not invalidate the fast.[33]

Several *fatāwā* deal with issues relating to women and their influence on the fast. Since menstruation renders the woman impure, therefore unable to fast, she is required by Islamic law to make up for the missed days of fasting at a later date. Fasting while menstruating is considered a sin.[34] Women who insist on performing the fast uninterruptedly have found that with the use of contraceptive pills and others too, they can postpone the menstrual period until after Ramadan.

It is obviously a convenience and not any medical justification, which stands behind this "device." Nevertheless, at least one *muftī* pronounced clear permission for this method. He understood the motive behind the deed to be religious devotion and the wish to perform the fast perfectly.[35]

Another *muftī* is ambiguous about it: on the one hand he prefers human physiology not to be artificially disrupted. On the other hand he recalls a precedent from the time of the Caliph Umar, who witnessed a woman taking pills to stop her period so she could set out on the *ḥajj*, but he did not condemn her attempt. Umar instead recommended a juice extracted from the *arāk* tree (*Salvadora Persica*) for the same purpose.[36]

A third *muftī*, however, was decidedly against the use of pills to delay menstruation. He claimed that the release by God of the menstruating woman and the woman after childbirth from the duty to fast was proof that the bodily cycle has a purpose. Islamic law is in harmony with the female body, and is against violating the body's natural behavior. Besides, pills can generate future diseases to the woman, and they are therefore prohibited.[37] Human beings are warned by Islamic theology against damaging their health and wellbeing.

Another question which concerns the contraceptive pill is if swallowing the pill during the days of Ramadan, even without drinking

---

[32] *Al-Liwā' Al-Islāmī*, April 12, 1990, p. 6 (a *fatwā* by 'Abd Al-Munṣif Maḥmūd); *Al-Muslimūn*, March 22, 1991, p. 8 (a *fatwā* by Muḥammad Sayyid Ṭanṭāwī).

[33] *Al-Jum'a*, May 1987, p. 4 (a *fatwā* by Sheikh 'Abd Al-Laṭīf Mushtaharī).

[34] *Al-Nūr*, July 5, 1989, p. 8 (a *fatwā* by 'Abd Al-Fattāḥ 'Āshūr).

[35] *Muftī* Muḥammad 'Alī 'Abd Al-Raḥīm, in: *Majallat Al-Tawḥīd*, no. 3, Rabī' Al-Awwal 1411, pp. 23-24.

[36] *Al-Jumhūriyya*, April 11, 1991, p. 7 (a *fatwā* by Dr. Abū Sarī' 'Abd Al-Hādī).

[37] *Al-Liwā' Al-Islāmī*, March 29, 1990, p. 17.

water, violates the fast. The answer is that it does, because the pill reaches the stomach through the mouth. A woman who took the pill during a day of Ramadan was recommended to fast another day instead of the day when she swallowed the pill.[38] Needless to say, there is no objection to the general idea of using contraceptive pills in this *fatwā*.

One woman asked whether bleeding that occurred two months after miscarriage was considered *nifās* (postnatal bleeding), in which case she must cease fasting, or not?

The answer was that any delivery or miscarriage followed by bleeding is equal to *nifās*, and the woman then is to observe the laws of *nifās*, i.e., no fast and no prayer. Missed days of fasting can be made up after the bleeding stops and the woman has performed *ghusl* (large ablution).[39]

With regard to dental care and hygiene, people often inquire if they may use toothbrush and toothpaste during Ramadan, since they dislike the bad odor which emanates from their mouth and stomach. The usual response is that as long as the paste does not enter the throat, and thence the stomach, it may be used. Washing the mouth with water that is not swallowed is permissible. The use of a *siwāk* (toothstick)—dry or moist—during Ramadan is generally accepted as legitimate.[40] It is nevertheless emphasized that the bad smell coming from the mouth of the fasting person during Ramadan is desired by God; it is a sign of religious devotion which must not be erased.[41]

In addition to the special medical aspects of prayer, *ḥajj* and fast, there are several general tenets that hold for all religious duties as well as for daily conduct, at all times, and therefore pertain to our present discussion. These are:

a. Medicines which contain alcohol for disinfective purposes or for dissolving the medicine are not considered intoxicants, and can therefore be used in any medical treatment. By analogy, French perfumes, which are used for both scent and medical disinfection, are also permitted.[42] Cologne water is allowed for ablution,

---

[38] *Al-Muslimūn*, April 5, 1991, p. 8 (issued by the Fatāwā Committee at Al-Azhar).

[39] *Al-Jumhūriyya*, March 8, 1991, p. 7 (a *fatwā* by Ra'fat Uthmān).

[40] Vardit Rispler-Chaim, "The *Siwāk*: A Medieval Islamic Contribution to Dental Care", in: *The Journal of the Royal Asiatic Society*, vol. 2, part I, April 1992, pp. 13-20.

[41] *Al-Ahrām*, June 11, 1984, p. 12 (*muftī* ʻAbd Al-Laṭīf Ḥamza); *Al-Liwā' Al-Islāmī*, March 29, 1990, p. 8.

[42] *Fatāwā Rashīd Riḍā*, 1st edition, Beirut 1971, v. 4, p. 1603. The *fatwā* was first published in *Al-Manār* in 1922.

even though it contains a percentage of alcohol, because it is prepared for the purpose of cleansing and disinfecting, not intoxication.[43]

b. Chloroform, which is used during surgery as an anesthetic, is also permitted, because it allows the surgeon to work uninterruptedly while the patient feels no pain. This is so even though chloroform can be as intoxicating as some narcotics.[44]

c. Wine for medical purposes, undesirable as wine is in Islam, based on Qur'an 2, 219; 5,90, and other verses, is permissible if an experienced doctor believes it to be the only possible cure.[45] The Shāfiʿīs are supposedly tolerant of wine as medicine.[46] If a person is choking, and the only available method to stop it is a glass of wine, this is permitted.[47] The principle of saving one's life is given priority over the prohibition of drinking wine. Beer, however, is not granted the same acceptance. "Doctors should discover better medications than beer," it is asserted.[48]

In sum, the guidelines on how to observe religious duties when sick are consistent and clear, and tend to appeal to logical justifications as well as to tested medical facts. Still, the border between the wish to fulfil a commandment and concern for one's health is not always that obvious. This is where the Muslim doctor is invoked to mark the priorities, and in a way to share the conscientious responsibility that a devout Muslim is reluctant to bear alone. The progress of medicine as indicated by new medications and medical devices renders the role of the *muftī* in formulating the medical ethics of religious worship even more indispensable.

---

[43] Sheikh Muḥammad Khāṭir, in: *Al-Liwā' Al-Islāmī*, July 18, 1991, p. 8.

[44] *Al-Umma Al-Islāmiyya*, September 1985, p. 8.

[45] Ḥasanayn Muḥammad Makhlūf, in: *Al-Fatāwā Al-Islāmiyya*, Cairo 1982, v. 7, p. 1073 (dated November 15, 1952).

[46] Yaʿqūbī, *Shifā' Al-ta'rīkh*, 1st edition, Damascus 1986, p. 85.

[47] *Al-Umma Al-Islāmiyya*, May 1985, p. 7; Sheikh Ibrāhīm Al-Yaʿqūbī, *Shifā' Al-Ta'rīkh*, p. 85.

[48] *Al-Umma Al-Islāmiyya*, February 1985, p. 7.

CHAPTER SEVEN

DOCTOR–PATIENT RELATIONS

Any discussion of medicine includes the role of the Muslim doctor in advising and persuading the Muslim patient to undergo or avoid a particular treatment, and in performing certain medical procedures.

It is widely acknowledged nowadays that the personality of the doctor and the trust a patient has in him/her is one very important component of the medical treatment itself and of the likelihood of illnesses being cured. It is of course desirable that the doctor also be learned, skilled, experienced, gentle, moral and compassionate. This is required of doctors anywhere, not only in Islamic societies. However, for the Muslim doctor and Muslim patient, there are more issues of concern, and these are related to the Islamic religious teachings and to their social derivatives.

Thus, as much as doctor-patient ethics in Islam touches upon the familiar cosmopolitan dilemma, such as the termination of life versus transplants and the saving of a mother's life by aborting her fetus, etc., it also discusses issues which are uniquely Islamic.

One typical question concerning doctor-patient relations is whether a male doctor can treat a female patient, or vice versa.

The segregation of males and females who are not related by marriage or blood ties (only certain degrees of blood ties), is required by Islamic law in order to protect the chastity of both sexes—*ʿawra*[1] (private body parts), but especially that of females.

Even when a female doctor examines a female patient, or a male doctor a male patient, they are required to overlook the patient's private body parts. This is meant to preserve the patient's dignity and right to privacy. When the doctor and patient are of opposite sexes, their being alone in a clinic also evokes the problem of the *khalwa*

---

[1] Frederick Mathewson Denny in the glossary to his book *An Introduction to Islam*, Macmillan Publishing Company, USA 1985, defines *ʿawra* on page 395 as "Literally 'genitals'. The portions of the body that should be properly covered; males—from navel to knees, females—all but the face, hands and feet (according to the strictest observance)."

(seclusion),[2] which only married couples or persons who have specific blood ties may enjoy.

When any other man and woman go into *khalwa* they risk being suspected of sexual offenses, they may be punished, and they often damage their reputation. In order to avoid unnecessary cases of *khalwa*, Muslims would often recommend the presence of a nurse, a female relative or the husband of the patient in the clinic, while the male doctor examines a woman. Some modernists, though, might condemn this phenomenon as an expression of sexual discrimination.[3]

Despite the concern with the social need to protect the *ʿawra* and to avoid *khalwa*, when there is no other option, on the principle that "necessities render the prohibitions permitted" men and women may be treated by doctors of the opposite sex as well.[4]

It is sometimes explained in this regard, that the doctor, who has dedicated his life to healing people, is unlikely to misuse his position and defame his profession. Besides, medicine calls for mercy and saving life, not for arousing temptation. Therefore, when necessary a male doctor can treat a woman, although it is always preferred that a female doctor treat her.[5] When a treatment is not medically urgent, a man may not examine a woman. Therefore, in a case of infertility of the woman, it was suggested that she wait until a female doctor is available to treat her. It was not viewed as a question of life and death.[6] But there are numerous examples of cases in which a male doctor was legally permitted to treat a woman. Obstetricians, even male and single, may deliver babies, even when the delivery is believed to be proceeding naturally; it cannot be predicted whether the delivery will be simple or complicated. The lives of both the mother and the fetus are at stake, and the presence of a specialist is therefore recommended; if no female doctor is available, a male obstetrician

---

[2] *khalwa*—a situation in which a man and a woman are both located in a closed place *alone*, and where sexual intercourse between them can occur. *Khalwa* is one condition for which the man owes the woman dower, even when the marriage contract has not yet been signed. See: ʿAbd al-Raḥmān Al-Jazīrī, *Kitāb Al-Fiqh ʿalā Al-Madhāhib Al-Arbaʿa*, Cairo 1990, v.4, pp. 95-96.

[3] Ahmed Elkadi, "Professional Ethics", in: *The Journal of Islamic Medical Association*, September 1976, pp. 27-30.

[4] ʿAṭiyya Ṣaqr, in: *Al-Ahrām*, February 15, 1985, p. 13; *Al-Nūr*, August 5, 1990, p. 7; *Al-Nūr*, July 25, 1990, p. 7; *Al-Muslimūn*, July 12, 1991, p. 8 (the permanent Fatāwā Committee in Saudi Arabia).

[5] *Al-Umma Al-Islāmiyya*, February 1985, p. 7.

[6] *Al-Muslimūn*, March 1, 1991, p. 8 (Sheikh ʿAbd Allah Al-Jabarīn).

should participate in any delivery.[7] In the same way, a male orthopedist, who sometimes has to measure the legs and arms of women to fit artificial limbs to the handicapped, is also permitted to do so, even though the *'awra* of the patients may unintentionally be exposed. A female orthopedist is of course preferable, but in her absence, a male orthopedist cannot be blamed for doing his job.[8]

More complicated is the *khalwa* of a male psychiatrist with a female patient. Unlike the previous cases, the nature of psychiatric treatment often requires that the doctor and patient are present alone in a room. The confidentiality created by this *khalwa* is essential for the success of the therapy, which may also last for a long period of time. Still, if this treatment is believed to help the patient and the male doctor is a devout Muslim, the *khalwa* is again legitimized and not perceived malicious.[9]

It is fitting that the doctor be a devout Muslim. This is probably based on the assumption that one has only one soul—only one ethical code. That means that professional ethics is only a reflection of personal ethics. Obviously, according to this philosophy, being a devout Muslim guarantees, a high standard of morality.[10]

If the male doctor is not a devout Muslim, it is recommended to consult a devout one, or a woman doctor. But if the non-devout doctor is the only specialist in the town, and the patient has confidence in him, it is nevertheless allowed to continue the treatment under the non-devout Muslim physician.[11]

The problem of forbidden mingling of women and men exists also with regard to the medical staff itself, i.e., female doctors and nurses who work beside male colleagues. In a fundamentalist journal it is emphasized that Muslim women may work, but only if dressed in Islamic garb and only in women's departments. The common counterclaim, that women in the early days of Islam used to treat men too, is believed true, but with the reservation that no one knows for sure what dress those women wore and if they exposed their beauty to the public eye.[12]

---

[7] Sheikh Ḥasan Ma'mūn in a *fatwā* dated October 16, 1957, which was published in *Al-Fatāwā Al-Islāmiyya*, v.7, pp. 2489-2490.

[8] Sheikh Ibrāhīm Al-Waqfī, in: *Al-Liwā' Al-Islāmī*, June 13, 1991, p. 6.

[9] Al-Sha'rāwī, *Mi'at Su'āl wa Jawāb*, Cairo n.d., pp. 9-10.

[10] Ahmed Elkadi, "Professional Ethics".

[11] Al-Sha'rāwī, *Al-Fatāwā*, Cairo 1981, v.8, p. 90.

[12] Sheikh 'Alī 'Abd Al-Raḥīm, in: *Majallat Al-Tawḥīd*, No. 9, Ramadan 1407, p. 31.

Muslims are often concerned by whether they may be treated by non-Muslim doctors. The problem is aggravated when the non-Muslim doctor is consulted on medical matters which impinge on Islamic religious worship.

One person relates, in this regard, that a Christian doctor who treated him for tuberculosis (*sill*) between 1948 and 1953, and who has since examined him every two or three months, recommended that the Muslim patient completely avoid fasting during Ramadan. The question is if this recommendation must be obeyed, or more specifically, if "Islam" is an essential condition in a doctor who is consulted about Muslims' ability to worship. Sheikh Makhlūf, who was approached on this problem, explained that the Ḥanafīs and Shāfi'is stipulated that the doctor be a Muslim; the Mālikīs, however, did not. Makhlūf suggested that for precaution, while in doubt whether there indeed exists a medical impediment in religious devotion, a skilled Muslim doctor must be approached, and his opinion then followed.[13]

The more liberal Mālikī point of view on consultation with a non-Muslim doctor, was adopted also in an interesting case in the USA. A 30-year-old single Muslim woman, a virgin, was hospitalized for growths found in her body. Later on, growths were discovered in her womb too. The removal of her hymen became inevitable in order to diagnose them. When the woman refused to undergo the operation, she was released from hospital to consult a Muslim doctor.

The main problem seems to have been the decision to remove the hymen —a mark of chastity for single Muslim women, which would definitely entail social and emotional complications for this young woman in the future. Arising from this is the question if a non-Muslim doctor is at all qualified to decide on such a crucial step.

To solve the problem it was suggested that a Muslim doctor opine on the case. But if no Muslim doctor could be found, a trustworthy non-Muslim doctor could be consulted as well. After all, to avoid any treatment, which might result in death, is forbidden in Islamic law as it borders on suicide.[14]

For female patients the following order of priorities is suggested: approach a female Muslim doctor; if one is not available, a male Muslim doctor, and only if neither is available, a non-Muslim doctor. The

---

[13] Makhlūf, *Fatāwā Shar'iyya wa Buḥūth Islāmiyya*, 3rd edition, Cairo 1971, v. 1, pp. 302-303.

[14] *Al-Liwā' Al-Islāmī*, March 29, 1990, p. 8.

latter option is legitimized under the principle of emergency, i.e., *al-ḍarūrāt tubīḥ Al-Maḥẓūrāt.*[15]

The responsibility of the Muslim doctor

The responsibility of the Muslim doctor stretches beyond purely medical issues. The Muslim doctor is often asked if a person can perform the religious duties of Islam without harm to his/her health. The duties most at issue are the fast of Ramadan and the *ḥajj*. These are the hardest to fulfil, and they also take place once a year and once a lifetime, respectively. Since the *ḥajj* and fast are fixed dates in the Islamic calendar and their performance is so highly revered, every devout Muslim strives not to omit them.

Islamic law allows the sick and people with certain disabilities, whether temporary or permanent, to miss days of the fast or even the whole fast, and to postpone the pilgrimage until they recover or until their financial situation improves (and until the political atmosphere improves), or forever. The law also includes provisions to compensate for the "lost" days of fasting and for the unfulfilled yet obligatory *ḥajj*.

The doctor is approached in the "border cases", i.e., cases of an on-going diseases such as a heart condition, where fasting may not be harmful but the patient worries that additional damage to his/her heart may nevertheless occur.[16]

In most cases, to free themselves from the heavy responsibility, doctors may advise their patients that "you know best how long you can tolerate the fast or carry on a pilgrimage. So you decide for yourself". But a doctor knows better than any patient the risks involved, and a devout Muslim doctor has sometimes to take a clear stand in either permitting or prohibiting the fulfilment of a duty. On the other hand, it is not acceptable that on account of any disease whatsoever doctors free their patients from the obligation to fulfil a religious duty.[17]

The Muslim doctor thus acts as a mediator between the medical and religious spheres; he has to be loyal to both and ensure that they complement each other, and not clash or cancel each other out.

---

[15] *Al-Jumʿa*, September-October 1989, p. 21; *Al-Taṣawwuf Al-Islāmī*, July 1981.

[16] Jād Al-Ḥaqq in a *fatwā* dated February 11, 1979, in: *Al-Fatāwā Al-Islāmiyya*, v.8, 1983, pp. 2781-2784.

[17] Dr. Mūsā Shāhīn Lāshīn, in: *Al-Jumhūriyya*, June 19, 1983, p. 5.

As is the case in Western medicine, the Muslim medical student also takes an oath before he/she starts to practice. The content of this oath is not new. It includes the pledge to care for the sick in the best possible way, to keep medical information confidential, etc. This oath is perceived to be as serious as any oath made under Islamic law (*yamīn*). This means that whenever any clause of the oath is breached, a ransom (*kafāra*) has to be paid by the doctor.[18] This is the only Islamic nuance of the Muslim doctor's oath.

Malpractice accusations are not only the Western doctor's concern. Some cases in which malpractice can be suspected derive directly from the Islamic lifestyle and Islamic law. Compensation due on malpractice is called *ḍamān* (guarantee), and is a recognized transaction in Islamic law.[19] The recurring question is whether the doctor, who acted with good intent, has to compensate the patient, or the patient's family, when an accident occurs or when the patient dies as a result of the medical treatment.

One field of medicine in which accidents seem to have recurred is that of circumcisions. What is the obligation of the circumciser then? The law provides contradictory answers to this question.

If a doctor performs circumcision on a man (*khitān*), and the man dies, the doctor is not liable for the death.[20] However, the caliph Umar obliged a person who performed circumcisions and cut part of the boy's penis to pay compensations.[21] Umar also required that a woman who used to circumcise females (*khafḍ*), and one of her patients suffocated as a result of it, pay *ḍamān*.[22]

The principle which seems to emerge from Islamic law is that whenever the doctor acts with good intent and no negligence can be shown in his/her conduct, but accidents and even deaths still occur for

---

[18] Sheikh Ḥasan Ma'mūn in a *fatwa* dated June 28, 1956, and published in *Al-Fatāwā Al-Islāmiyya*, v.6, 1982, pp. 2085-2086. For the cases of breaking an oath for which *kafāra* is required, see for example: 'Abd Al-Raḥmān Al-Jazīrī, *Al-Fiqh 'Alā Al-Madhāhib Al-Arba'a*, Cairo 1990, v. 2, pp. 67-68.

[19] See: Vardit Rispler-Chaim, "Insurance and Semi-Insurance Transactions in Islamic History Until the 19th Century", in: *Journal of the Economic and Social History of the Orient*, vol. 34, pp. 142-158, fn. 10.

[20] See: "ḍamān al-ṭabīb", in: *Al-Fatāwā Al-Islāmiyya*, v. 7, Cairo 1982, pp. 2412-2415, based on *Ḥāshiyat Al-Dasūqī* (whose author died in 1814).

[21] *Muṣannaf 'Abd Al-Razzāq*, 1st edition, Lebanon 1972, v.9, pp. 470-472.

[22] Ibid.

unforeseeable reasons, the doctor is free of malpractice charges, hence of any financial obligation.[23]

However, when the doctor has violated one of the following conditions:

a. he was not fully licensed (even when damage has not yet been indicated!)
b. he did not obtain the patient's permission to treat him/her (except for cases in which the ruler authorizes a doctor to amputate the hand of a thief, etc.
c. the doctor was negligent
d. the doctor operated on the body beyond the location agreed by the patient.[24]

—In these conditions, the doctor is held liable, and has therefore to compensate for the damages.

By analogy, if a doctor performed urological surgery, for example, and the sexual functioning of the patient consequently declined, the doctor is not liable.[25]

It is worth mentioning in this regard that in the Middle Ages too the Muslim jurists debated the requirement that doctors pay compensations when they erred in the treatment offered, in diagnosing the disease, or in assessing the health of the patient. The reasons then were:

a. if doctors feared high fines and heavy financial punishments, they would refuse to treat patients unless they were absolutely sure that the remedy was suitable.
b. mistakes contribute to medical science.
c. caring for the sick is a divine decree; therefore, only negligent doctors must be punished, not those who acted with good intent but erred.[26]

Sheikh Abū Zuhra of Al-Azhar surveyed four cases in which a skilled doctor's action can lead to total or partial damage to the body:

---

23 Ibid.

24 *Al-Fatāwā Al-Islāmiyya*, v. 7, 1982, pp. 2412-2415.

25 Ibid.

26 Muḥammad Abū Zuhra, "mas'ūliyyat al-ṭabīb", in: *Liwā' Al-Islām*, April 1949, pp. 52-53, and May 1949, pp. 53-57.

a. when a doctor failed to consider some aspect, because based on his experience and assessment it was not important. This is not a case of negligence, not even a mistake.
b. the doctor erred; for example, he made more incisions than necessary.
c. the doctor prescribed the wrong medicine, and
d. the patient did not give permission for the treatment which led to the physical damage.

Following the 14th-century jurist Ibn Qayyim, Abū Zuhra agrees that no *ḍamān* is due from the doctor in any of these cases.[27]

However, *bayt al-māl* (The Treasury) should compensate the patient or his/her family so as to demonstrate that no Muslim's blood is violable. Also, since doctors, like judges, are public officials, they merit protection by the state. This is meant to encourage doctors to willingly treat patients, and not to fear evil consequences which are beyond their control.[28]

This Islamic approach, which some may view as a shield for unskilled doctors, should also be weighed against the over-preoccupation of Western medicine with malpractice claims, which leads to high costs of physicians' malpractice insurance. This, in turn, is translated into high costs of medical services and hence their availability to the wealthy only. Another result of the constant worry about malpractice charges is that doctors are reluctant to take medically complicated cases.

Despite the unique problems which the Muslim doctor and patient may encounter in their mutual search for a cure, the First International Conference on Islamic Medicine (held in Kuwait in January 1981) drew up the *Islamic Code of Medical Ethics*, which surprisingly included *no* clause which is solely Islamic. It encourages the doctor to be gentle with the sick and their family members or friends. It emphasizes that health is a basic human need, not a luxury. Thus poor people are entitled to be treated as well. However, in private practice, the doctor has the right to fix his/her fees.[29] Doctors should be able to live respectably from their profession, provided they maintain high

---

[27] Ibid.
[28] Ibid.
[29] *Islamic Code of Medical Ethics*, p. 44.

standards.[30] All information provided by the patient, whether heard, seen or understood by the doctor, should be kept secret by the doctor.[31]

The acceptance of the doctor by the patient is held as acceptance of all the treatments this particular doctor offers. As for surgery, the doctor's decision must be signed, and if the patient refuses to receive a certain treatment this should be noted in a document signed by him/her too.[32] If the patient is afraid of a remedy, it is the task of the doctor to reassure and convince him/her. It is forbidden to give the patient any treatment which could lead to his/her losing consciousness and hence the ability to make choices.[33]

In times of emergency the doctor must act according to his/her understanding and training, for the purpose of saving life. The results of such emergency treatment are protected by the principle "necessities render the prohibitions permitted."[34]

Terminally ill patients should remain under full health care, with moral support and without pain and suffering. The patient always has the right to know what his/her illness is. The exact manner of disclosure should be adjusted to each individual patient.[35] Much emphasis is laid on maintaining the rights of the patient as a human being: the right to privacy, to make choices, to decide of his/her future, to live in dignity and so to die. Likewise, with regard to the doctors it is reminded time and again that they should be trusted and that they are human beings in addition to their being professionals, hence they

---

[30] Ibid., p. 45. This contemporary view of doctors' payment seems to be more or less prevalent. In the Middle Ages, however, there existed a debate on whether doctors should charge patients at all. Some doctors were reported to live off commerce, and did not need to ask for payment for their medical services. This raised another dilemma, of whether the sidelines did not distract doctors from concentrating on the medical knowledge; so medicine should pay like any other profession.

Based on Hypocrates, life-saving is priceless, and therefore no remuneration to the doctor is ever adequate. Greek medical ethics in general differentiated between the respect held for medicine and the financial needs of the doctor. Contrary to that, in the Jewish book *Sefer Musar Rofīm* by Isaac Israeli (ed. 955) it was suggested that the rich should pay "more than enough", so that the poor might obtain free treatment. See: H.H. Biesterfeldt, "Some Opinions on the Physicians Remuneration in Medieval Islam", *Bulletin of the History of Medicine*, vol.58, No. 1, 1984, pp. 16-27.

[31] *Islamic Code of Medical Ethics*, p. 49.

[32] Ibid., p. 58.

[33] Ibid.

[34] Ibid., p. 59.

[35] Ibid., p. 68.

might err. However, it is repeated that they usually act out of good intention and should therefore be encouraged to continue their blessed work, and not be condemned for each mistake they might perform.

Despite the "semi-secular" content of the *Islamic Code of Medical Ethics*, one must not ignore the fact that it is nevertheless entitled "Islamic". Although not overtly stated, we think it is implied that the reference to Allah and the recognition by every Muslim that there is a divine God who supervises all things, including the actions of doctors, are likely to engender greater humility in doctors, more careful practice, and hence more ethical medicine. Dr. Elkadi goes further, to conclude that any ethical system which is not somehow related to God, i.e., a system which is only man-made, is likely to suffer from errors. The Islamic system, which draws on the Qur'an, is decidedly not solely man-made. It must therefore be better.[36]

---

[36] Ahmed Elkadi, "Professional Ethics."

CHAPTER EIGHT

POSTMORTEM EXAMINATIONS

Very little has been written on postmortems in the 20th century, however, in the second half of the 20th century the subject of postmortems has been discussed by Muslim scholars more than in the past, as it has been by Western thinkers and by scholars of other religions too.

Due to the rapid development of medicine in the 20th century and to the development of its scientific methods, postmortems have become an efficient instrument to learn more of the causes of death, and consequently of ways to postpone death in certain cases. In many modern states postmortems are mandatory in order to verify the cause of death; as such they have proved helpful in solving criminal deaths and in bringing about justice.

For religious people, postmortems may seem a desecration of the human body. For monotheists, at least, the body is viewed as God's property deposited with a human being for a limited period after which it should be returned to God in the best condition possible. No changes, omissions or additions are allowed. Therefore, Jews and Christians share with Muslims a similar sensitivity to questions such as transplant of body parts, donation of body parts and postmortems.

Ḥasanayn Muḥammad Makhlūf's *fatwa* on postmortems is the most comprehensive on the issue. Therefore, it will be studied in detail.[1] Makhlūf was born in Cairo in 1890, appointed qadi in 1916, head of the Sharʿī court in Alexandria in 1941 and chief Muftī of Egypt in 1945. From 1948 he also served as a member of the Supreme Council of scholars at Al-Azhar[2] (the university for Islamic studies in Cairo). His opinion can be regarded as representative of mainstream Sunni Islam. Other contemporary scholars' views of postmortems will also be studied for comparison.

---

[1] It appeared in: Makhlūf, Ḥ.M., *Fatāwā Sharʿiyya wa Buḥūth Islāmiyya*, Cairo 1952, pp. 219-224.

[2] The personal data appear at the beginning of the third edition of his book, Cairo: Al-Madanī, 1971.

Makhlūf's fatwā *on postmortem examinations*

The exact question as presented to Makhlūf is if postmortems are permitted for scientific purposes and for the solving of criminal cases. The question is not a general one, of if the Sharīʿa approves of postmortems at all, but rather of their legitimacy for certain specified purposes—those that to a Western reader at least sound justified, humane and indispensable.

The responsum starts with a wider topic, medicine as a whole, and the high esteem it was granted in the Sharīʿa, especially since the Prophet treated himself medically and encouraged his Companions to seek cures for their diseases. In addition to the historic practice of the Prophet, Makhlūf finds further support for the importance of medicine in Islamic life; many concessions were allowed already in the Qur'an for sick people, granting priority to the preservation of their good health over the observance of God's commandments when the latter posed a danger to it.

Moreover, the practice of medicine was recognized as so essential for Islamic society that it was listed by the Sharīʿa among *furūḍ al-kifāyāt* (obligations of sufficiency), thus requiring that there always be a sufficient number of people to practice it; as such it was equated with the duty of *jihād* (holy war) and with the duty to attend funerals. Medicine, which is viewed nowadays as a scientific and secular occupation, was definitely endowed with a religious dimension by the Sharīʿa.

Only at this point does Makhlūf touch upon postmortems, and he does so using the following analogy: since medicine is so essential for Islamic society, and since a doctor cannot become competent unless he has learned all the internal and external parts of the human body, something which can be achieved only by a postmortem, one must conclude that postmortems are essential for a progressive knowledge of medicine to develop.

Makhlūf goes on to refute one possible counterclaim, namely that medicine survived hundreds of years without resorting to postmortems, by saying that ancient medicine was primitive and responded only to external symptoms, while modern medicine is required to answer all problems and to utilize contemporary science and technology.

Postmortems are thus viewed by Makhlūf as an inseparable part of a doctor's education, just as ablution is an integral part of the commandment to pray. Hence he established the importance of postmortems for purely scientific considerations beyond any doubt.

Makhlūf justifies the use of a postmortem to solve criminal cases on the basis of ensuring justice, acquitting the innocent and convicting the guilty. This is an appeal to the natural sense of justice.

He goes on to defend postmortems against the charge that they violate the sanctity of the human body. Here Makhlūf resorts to the useful principle in Islamic theological reasoning that whenever benefits outnumber damages a positive approach should be taken (*maṣlaḥa*). Consequently, since postmortems result in more benefits than damages, the Sharīʿa may be in favor of them.

Makhlūf finally relies on a previous *fatwā* on the same issue given by Sheikh Yūsuf Al-Dajawī, who also legitimized postmortems on the basis of *maṣlaḥa*. Al-Dajawī compared the case of violating human dignity in postmortems with the approved permission in the Sharīʿa to remove money from a dead person's belly. Analogously, Al-Dajawī concluded that in postmortems the damage to the body was more excusable and the benefit much greater.

Makhlūf closes his *fatwā* with Al-Dajawī's statement that doctors, politicians and the public in general should be God-fearing and perform postmortems only when necessary.

Although in his *fatwā* Makhlūf does not mention specific Sharīʿa references, certain points in his responsum can easily be grounded in Sharʿī topics. Those that seem most relevant to postmortems are the following.

1. High esteem has indeed been reserved in the Sharīʿa for medicine since the time of the Prophet. Ibn Qayyim Al-Jawziya (d. 1350) related that the Prophet recommended treating the sick by day and by night. A Muslim who tends the sick is blessed with the company of 70,000 angels who pray for him/her day and night.[3] A similar tradition was mentioned by Ibn Qudāma (d. 1223).[4] It appears already in the Hadith collections that the Prophet stated that each sickness was revealed accompanied by its cure.[5] This is intended to encourage sick people and the doctors to seek that cure. From here we learn of the important role the doctor plays: it is he who mediates and delivers the remedy revealed by God to

[3] Ibn Qayyim, *Zād Al-Maʿād*, Cairo 1970, v. 1, p. 170.
[4] Ibn Qudāma, *Al-Mughnī*, Beirut 1972, v. 2, p. 303.
[5] Ibn Qayyim, *Zād Al-Maʿād*, v. 1, p. 78.

those who are in need of it.[6] Although God is the source of the sickness as well as remedy, the doctor is essential to deliver the remedy. Makhlūf indirectly acknowledges the contribution of postmortems to the discovery of new remedies.

2. Further support for the importance which the Sharīʿa attributes to medicine can be deduced from the many concessions which God allowed in the observance of religious duties in order not to jeopardize health. In other words, the law concerning religious duties already includes permission not to perform that duty if the medical condition of the believer so requires. The law also specifies monetary or other compensation instead of a religious duty that is not completely fulfilled. During Ramadan, for example, the fast can be abandoned if for some reason a person cannot eat at daybreak. According to another instruction, whenever fasting is physically harmful it is obligatory to stop it. Therefore the elderly, the permanently thirsty, pregnant women and nursing mothers whose milk is scanty can forgo the fast. Instead, they should give alms in the form of some portion of food to the poor for each day of the fast they miss. When their physical condition improves they are expected to make good the missing days of fasting.[7] The inference here is that when health requirements contradict Islamic law, as may be in the case of postmortems, health is given priority.
3. According to Makhlūf, medicine is so highly esteemed by the Sharīʿa that its practice and learning won it the status of *farḍ kifāya*, i.e., a duty which unless performed by a certain number of Muslim participants is not considered fulfilled. Only when that number is reached may the rest of the community view itself exempt, for the goal has been achieved.[8] We are more used to hearing about joining a *jihād* (holy war), following a funeral, performing ablution and of burying the dead as *farḍ kīfāyā* than about practicing medicine. According to Makhlūf it is now an obligation rather than an option for the community to provide a sufficient number of physicians. Consequently, if there must be doctors they

---

[6] *Zād Al-Maʿād*, v. 1, p. 80.

[7] Ibn Bābawayhi (d. 991), *Man lā Yaḥḍuruhu Al-Faqīh*, Najf 1957, v. 2, pp. 83-84.

[8] For the definition of *farḍ kifāya*, see: Al-Kāsānī (d. 1191), *Badā ʾiʿ Al-Ṣanāʾiʿ*, Cairo 1966, v. 2, pp. 751-766; Al-Tūrkmānī Al-Ḥanafī (14th century), *Kitāb Al-Lumaʿ*, Cairo 1986, v. 1, p. 219.

had better be skilled, which leads Makhlūf to his conclusion that the practice of postmortems produces better doctors.

4. Makhlūf is aware of the biggest fear of postmortem examinations: they might violate the sanctity of the body, especially when autopsy is involved. Makhlūf cannot deny here that postmortems indeed involve dissecting the body, and to a certain degree violate its wholeness. He admits that the deceased should be respected and their rights should be upheld even after death.

This is in agreement with the Sharīʿa. The Shīʿī Al-Ṭūsī (d. 1068) states that "the status of a deceased person is like that of a fetus and they even bear the same *diya* (blood money) when harmed. Whoever causes physical damage to the deceased, damage that if caused to a living person could have killed him, must pay 100 dinars. If he breaks the deceased's hand or amputates it, pulls out an eye or wounds it, he has to pay the due blood money on these damages, exactly as if he had damaged body parts of a living person."[9]

The Ḥanbalī Ibn Qudāma encourages the treatment of the dead with care in preparation for burial, in order to respect them, because they should be treated like the living, and because whoever amputates any body-part from the dead deserves like treatment. The Prophet's saying "breaking a bone of the deceased is like breaking a bone of a living person" is often quoted in this context.[10] Ibn Qudāma includes the harm done to the deceased within the realm of Islamic criminal law which is very strict, involves physical punishments and therefore successful as a deterrent.

The Mālikī Ibn Al-Ḥāj (d. 1336) states: "Anything which does not suit a Muslim while alive, should not be done to him/her after his/her death, except for what the Sharīʿa permitted."[11] It is left to Makhlūf now to prove that postmortems have aspects in them which fall within "what the Sharīʿa permitted".

5. Cases are mentioned in the Sharīʿa that we might define as "postmortems" today: in certain cases the Sharīʿa permitted the opening of a cadaver's belly to remove money from it. According to Ibn Qudāma, if before his death a person swallowed a large

[9] Al-Ṭūsī, *Al-Nihāya fī Mujarrad Al-Fiqh wal-Fatāwā*, Beirut 1970, p. 779. The same idea appears also in Al-Muḥaqiq, Al-Ḥillī *Sharāʾiʿ Al-Islām, Al-Fiqh Al-Islāmī Al-Jaʿfarī*, Beirut 196-, v. 2, p. 309.

[10] Ibn Qudāma, *Al-Mughnī*, v. 2, p. 323.

[11] Ibn Al-Ḥāj, *Al-Madkhal*, Cairo 1960, 3:253.

> amount of money belonging to another, his belly could be cut open and the money recovered even after death. This is intended to return the money to its true owner and to free the heirs of the deceased from future possible claims against their inheritance.[12] It is worth noting that the same Ḥanbalīs debate if it is permitted to incise the belly of a deceased woman to retrieve a fetus. Mālikīs and Shāfiʿīs encourage doing so if the fetus is believed to be alive because they believe that a part of the deceased is sacrificed to prolong life, and it is therefore permitted. They too draw an analogy from the permission to remove money from a deceased person's belly, stating that life is worth more than money. By contrast, the Ḥanbalīs doubt that the fetus has a chance of survival, which thus renders the opening of its deceased mother's belly a violation of the body's sanctity.[13]

The lack of an absolute decision in the Sharʿī sources with regard to this last point allows for Makhlūf's concluding remark that it is permitted to perform postmortem examinations, but only when indeed necessary.

Other contemporary fatāwā *on postmortem examinations*

In 1910 the famous Egyptian scholar Rashīd Riḍā (d. 1935) published a *fatwā* entitled "postmortem examinations and the postponement of burial"[14] which seems to have been the first treatment of the topic in this century. Except for Makhlūf's *fatwā*, prior to 1950s we find little mention of postmortems in Islamic legal literature. The topic was evoked again in the last decade in response to the increasing use of postmortems in Western-style hospitals in Islamic and Arab countries. Thus, Riḍā's dealing with this subject remains unique, and indeed remarkable, against the silence of other *muftī*s regarding postmortems during the first decades of the century. The fact that Riḍā's *fatwā* was primarily of a political import may partly explain his early interest in the subject. This political aspect will be mentioned below.

The next major treatise on postmortems was Makhlūf's, probably composed in the 1940s. After that we find several *fatāwā* on postmortems only from the 1980s.

---

12 *Al-Mughnī*, v. 2, p. 414.
13 *Al-Mughnī*, v. 2, p. 413.
14 *Al-Manār*, 1910, v. 13, pp. 100-102.

The entire problem of if postmortem examinations are legitimized by contemporary Islamic law might be better answered if divided into the following sub-questions:

a. Should a burial be postponed so that a postmortem may be conducted?
b. Should a human body be transferred from place to place before its burial?
c. Do postmortems involve a violation of the sanctity associated in Islamic theology with the human body?
d. Is it permitted to perform postmortems for scientific purposes and for criminal identification?

a. *The postponement of burial*

Since postmortems require time, burial must necessarily be postponed. This poses a problem for religious Muslims, since the Sharīʿa encourages the burial of the dead as soon after death as possible, "in order to bring the dead person closer to what God has prepared for him/her." ʿAbd Al-Ḥalīm Maḥmūd (d. 1978), who was Sheik Al-Azhar in 1973-1978, states that any delay in burial is held against those responsible for it, and they are considered sinners. The only delay allowed is the time necessary for ablution and for the preparation of the body for burial.[15]

Riḍā dwelled on the aspect of verifying that the person considered dead was indeed dead. To prevent tragic accidents in which an unconscious person is mistaken for dead and is buried, Riḍā agreed to a delay in burial so that a doctor's medical examination could take place. Aware that hastiness in burials may lead to fatal mistakes, Riḍā allowed some extension of the time between death and burial.[16] Riḍā followed the same reasoning to conclude that when a non-Islamic government made a medical examination to verify death, mandatory, thus causing a delay in burial, it should not be viewed as an anti-Muslim measure but should have been appreciated and understood by Muslims as a blessed precaution. In other words, Muslims living in a non-Islamic state were not obliged to migrate to the Ottoman Empire to escape the law causing a delay in burial.

---

15 *Fatāwā ʿAbd Al-Ḥalīm Maḥmūd*, Cairo 1986, v. 2, p. 277.
16 *Fatāwā Rashīd Riḍā*, Beirut 1970, v. 3, pp. 851-853.

The two somewhat contradictory opinions, by Riḍā on the one hand and by Maḥmūd on the other, can both claim support in the Sharīʿa. On the one hand it is encouraged to hasten burial as an expression of respect for the dead and of bringing God's servant closer to Him.[17] A prompt burial ensures that the body does not lose its human form before its burial, and hence its human dignity.[18] It is also beneficial to the members of the community; if good fortune awaits the deceased, then the good deed of expediting the deceased to the Lord could be credited to them, and if the deceased was a bad person, they had better free themselves of his/her presence as soon as possible.[19]

On the other hand, if death is not established absolutely and beyond any doubt it is recommended to act more cautiously. Al-Shāfiʿī (d. 820), already in the second century of Islam recommended waiting two or three days before burial when someone was believed dead as a result of drowning or being struck by a storm. He explained that unconsciousness and a shock were common to people hit by a storm, attacked by wild beasts, shattered by war or who had fallen off a cliff. If they did not regain consciousness in two or three days, they were probably dead.[20] Ibn Qudāma limited the postponement until the usual physical signs of death appeared.[21] The Shāfiʿī Ibn Ḥajar Al-Haythamī (d. 1567) allowed a short delay in burial until camphor (*kāfūr*) to wash the deceased was obtained. The deceased, he claimed, deserved the best treatment.[22] Recently, Makhlūf himself permitted the donation of one's body for science, either by the deceased himself/herself prior to death, or by relatives' authorization.[23] In such cases, for the public benefit, burial is postponed almost indefinitely, and this is indeed revolutionary for Islamic law.

b. *Transferring the body from place to place*

Postmortems also require the transfer of a body from the residence of the deceased or from the site of death to a laboratory or hospital

17 Al-Turkmānī, *Kitāb Al-Lumaʿ*, v. 1, p. 219; Ibn Qayyim, *Zād Al-Maʿād*, v. 1, p. 171.

18 Ibn Qudāma, *Al-Mughnī*, v. 2, p. 307.

19 Ibn ʿĀbidīn (d. 1889), *Ḥāshiyat Radd Al-Muḥtār*, Beirut 196-, v. 1, p. 597.

20 Al-Shāfiʿī, *Kitāb Al-Umm*, Cairo 1961, v. 1, p. 277.

21 *Al-Mughnī*, v. 2, p. 208.

22 Ibn Ḥajar Al-Haythamī, *Al-Fatāwā Al-Kubrā Al-Fiqhiyya*, Cairo 1938, v. 2, p. 2.

23 *Al-Ahrām*, January 26, 1990, p. 13.

where the examination can take place. This may cause a delay in burial and possibly also physical damage leading to desecration of the body.

In the Sharīʿa we indeed find that it is preferred to bury the dead at the site of their death or killing, i.e., in the cemetery of the nearest community. Therefore, the Prophet ordered the interment of those slain in the battle of Uḥud (625) near the battlefield, although the cemetery of the city of Al-Madīna was not too distant. For the same reason, the conquerors of Damascus were buried where they fell, and not all of them at one site.[24] ʿĀʾisha, the beloved wife of the Prophet, condemned the transfer of her brother ʿAbd Al-Raḥmān b. Abī Bakr who died in Abyssinia to Mecca, knowing that the long journey could cause a deterioration of the body.[25]

Transferring of the deceased a distance of one or two miles is acceptable to the Sharīʿa, because most cemeteries are located that far from their respective towns.[26]

Aḥmad b. Ḥanbal (d. 855), however, permitted the transfer of the deceased any distance, if it was for "a justified purpose".[27] Such a view can speak for postmortems, as it allows the transfer of the deceased without limiting the distance. Since distance can be translated into terms of time too, Ibn Ḥanbal's view allows for the required delay in burial which postmortems entail.

We could not find in contemporary *fatāwā* a direct reference on the transfer of the dead immediately after their death. Two *fatāwā*, however, mention the transfer of a body after it had already been buried. In one, the transfer was permitted in order to prevent the body from being submerged in a flood; in another, so that family members would be able to visit the grave more often.[28] In both cases the ruling did not indicate a licence to transfer remains generally but was an ad hoc solution to a specific problem.

In another *fatwa*, the remains of the dead were allowed to be exhumed and transferred to a new cemetery, when the old one had not

---

[24] Ibn ʿĀbidīn, *Ḥāshiyat Radd Al-Muḥtār*, v. 1, p. 602. *Al-Nūr*, March 13, 1991, p. 7, repeats the same idea.

[25] Ibn Qudāma, *Al-Mughnī*, v. 2, p. 390; *Al-Nūr*, March 13, 1991, p. 7.

[26] Ibn ʿĀbidīn, *Ḥāshiyat Radd Al Muḥtār*, v. 1, p. 602.

[27] Ibn Qudāma, Al- Mughni, v. 2, p. 390.

[28] A *fatwā* issued by Sheikh ʿAbd Al-Ḥakīm Naʿnāʿ, in: *Al-Jumhūriyya*, August 13, 1984, p. 7, and a *fatwā* issued by ʿAbd Al-Ḥamīd Al-Sayyid Shāhīn and ʿAlī Ḥāmid ʿAbd Al-Raḥīm, in: *Majallat Al-Azhar*, September-October 1988, pp. 183-184.

been in use for over a century, and the site was earmarked for construction of a mosque.[29] Recently permission was issued to transfer the mummified bodies of the last Ottoman Sultan ʿAbd Al-Majīd and his wife from France to be buried in an Islamic state—Egypt. This was allegedly based on Ḥanafī ruling to the benefit of both the living and the dead.[30]

If an analogy can be applied here, the question is if the opening of a grave to transfer a body to a different site for any of the acceptable reasons listed is more serious a matter than the transfer of newly-deceased persons to a hospital for postmortems before they are buried? Needless to say, no such analogy has been drawn in contemporary *fatāwā*.

c. *Violation of the sanctity of the body*

Any operation on a human body that cannot cure it may fall into the category of desecration of the dead. This is the major problem that postmortems pose for religious people. Such examinations may at best benefit the living by contributing to their better understanding of the cause of death or date of death. The deceased cannot be helped by that. We must therefore consider if a postmortem is indeed a purposeless violation of the wholeness of the body.

Sheik ʿAbd Al-Fattāḥ stated that "any harm done to the deceased, such as the sale of his/her body or part of it, is considered damage to his/her dignity, and this is a major sin.[31]

The Sharīʿa adheres to the principle that "breaking the bone of a deceased is similar to breaking the bones of a living person". Analogously, the removal of any part of a cadaver (as may be the procedure in certain postmortems) is forbidden. According to one opinion, even circumcision is considered a removal of a body part and therefore illegitimate. (Obviously this opinion belongs to a minority of jurists only, and circumcisions are a common ritual for males, and in certain places for females as well). The removal of gold from one's teeth after death is permitted only if this does not lead to loss of the tooth.[32]

---

29 The *fatwā* was published both by ʿAbd Al-Ḥamīd Al-Sayyid Shāhīn and Ṣafwat ʿAbd Al-Jawād, in: *Majallat Al-Azhar*, August-September 1988, p. 84.

30 *Al-Liwāʾ Al-Islāmī*, September 12, 1991, p. 8 (a *fatwā* by Makhlūf).

31 *Al-Ahrām*, April 15, 1983, p. 13.

32 Ibn Qudāma, *Al-Mughnī*, v. 2, p. 326.

If a body part is found after the body has already been interred, that part should be washed separately and prayed for, and then buried beside the body in the same grave, although exposure of the body itself is not necessary.

A pregnant woman's belly should not be cut open when she dies, even when a living fetus is believed to exist. The fetus will be retrieved, if at all, by pressure applied by midwives on the belly or by their extraction of the fetus. If women are not available, men may not perform this task, and the mother will be left unburied until it is clear that the fetus is dead too. Only the Shāfiʿī's permit the incision of the dead mother's belly to retrieve a living fetus, by analogy with the occasional permission to retrieve money from a deceased's belly,[33] as already described. The Ḥanbalīs view any attempt to rescue the fetus as a desecration of one human body for an unreal chance of saving another.[34]

For all the reasons mentioned so far, the general Sharʿī position should be opposed to all postmortems. However, under one Sharʿī maxim—"needs render prohibitions permitted"—a pragmatic solution is reached: a postmortem may be performed on someone killed in a car accident when he/she is anonymous.[35] Does anonymity in this case guarantee that the hasty Islamic burial could not have been performed to begin with? Or that no relative may later claim that the dignity of the deceased was not properly maintained? An explanation is not provided, but this is at least a partial concession in the direction of legitimizing a few postmortems without violating Islamic law.

d. *Scientific purposes and criminal identification*

Postmortems for purely scientific purposes or to obtain justice by correctly identifying the cause of death "suffer" from all the abovementioned arguments: a delay in burial, the transfer of the body from one place to another before letting it rest in peace, and the possible violation of the wholeness of the body. Yet the answer of the *muftī*s is usually positive, based on balancing damages against benefits.

The *Fatāwā* Committee at Al-Azhar concluded in January 1982 that if medical students learn from postmortems, if justice will prevail

---

33 Ibn Qudāma, *Al-Mughnī*, v. 2, p. 413.

34 Ibid.

35 *Al-Ahrām*, April 15, 1983, p. 13.

through them and if contagious diseases can be controlled through them, then benefits indeed outnumber damages, provided that these examinations are performed only when necessary.[36]

Riḍā justified medical examinations of the dead to verify death, and was even ready to acquiesce to a foreign government's unacceptable law ordering it, at the expense of ignoring the general Islamic rule on the issue, in order not to risk the fatal mistake of burying a person alive.[37]

Again commonsense won out: positive elements were weighed against negative. The drive to approve postmortems by Riḍā was neither educational nor juridical, but purely humane.

Sheik ʿAbd Al-Fattāḥ allowed postmortems for teaching purposes on an anonymous person killed in a car crash, relying on the same principle of "needs render prohibitions permitted".[38]

We may summarize the above by saying that although postmortems involve elements unacceptable to Islamic law the benefits they provide are now considered indispensable. The unacceptable elements are excused on the grounds of the pragmatic Islamic legal principle of "the public benefit" (*maṣlaḥa*).

---

[36] *Majallat Al-Azhar*, January 1982, p. 650; *Al-Liwāʾ Al-Islāmī*, August 22, 1991, p. 7 (Sheikh Ibrāhīm Al-Waqfī).

[37] *Fatāwā Rashīd Riḍa*, Beirut 1970, v. 3, pp. 851-853.

[38] *Al-Ahrām*, April 15, 1983, p. 13.

CHAPTER NINE

CIRCUMCISION

One of the most controversial topics in medical ethics in Islam is circumcision (*khitān*). The reason is that there is no reference in the Qur'an for the obligation to perform circumcision. With regard to males, all that is mentioned in the Hadith is that Ibrāhīm circumcised himself (*ikhtatana*),[1] and that it is a *sunna.*

With regard to female circumcision (*khafḍ* or *khitān al-unthā*) the problem is even more complex. The hadiths which do mention female circumcision evaluate the practice in very wide terms, not clarifying if female circumcision is obligatory from a religious point of view, and if it is, what it involves in practice.

There is no doubt that female circumcision is practiced today, although views vary as to how common the custom actually is. The feminist movement among Muslim women which in recent years has grown more popular and vociferous, has served to bring the subject of female circumcision to public awareness and debate, especially as an aspect of human rights.[2]

As will be explained below, circumcision, and especially female circumcision, is probably a derivative of ancient and non-Islamic customs in various parts of the world. Therefore, one cannot discuss female circumcision without consideration of the delicate interweaving and mutual influence between Islamic law and customary law, a relationship which continues well into the present.

All types of circumcision adhere to one general tenet, namely that religious scholars have never viewed circumcision as a sort of castration, for this is strictly forbidden in all monotheistic religions. If circumcision had ever appeared to be some sort of castration, no monotheistic religion would have approved of it,[3] Islam being no exception.

---

[1] Muḥammad Anwar Al-Dīwabandī, *Fayḍ Al-Bārī ʿalā Ṣaḥīḥ Al-Bukhārī*, 1st edition, South Africa and India 1938, v. 4, p. 33.

[2] See for example Nawal El Saadawi's book *The Hidden Face of Eve*, translated and edited by Dr. Sherif Hetata, London 1980, in which she devotes a chapter to various aspects of the circumcision of girls, in order to denounce the practice.

[3] Al-Sayyid Muḥammad ʿĀshūr, *Al-Khitān fī Al-Sharāʾiʿ Al-Samāwiyya wal-Waḍʿiyya*, Cairo 1981, p. 30.

This is obviously an outcome of the theological perception that the body of a living person should never the harmed, unless the harm is intentional and shown to be essential for the recovery of that person.[4] The sanctity attributed to the human body, therefore, dictates that circumcisions must be performed only in the proven belief that they promote bodily health. No other motivation is acceptable.

Female circumcision, however, may put this progressive principle in jeopardy: it is sometimes related that Hagar, Abraham's second wife, was the first woman to undergo circumcision, but this was as a punishment demanded by Abraham's jealous first wife, Sarah.[5] As much as the punitive element is deprecated by the jurists as an argument in support of female circumcision, it still arouses suspicion that it exists, at least partially; the need in men to control female sexuality is sometimes satisfied by causing damage to female sexual organs.[6]

But male circumcision is described as a sign of adulthood and of joining the community of pious Muslim men, an act of allegiance and a symbol of purity. Therefore, most jurists appear unanimous that Muslim men must be circumcised (*wājib*).[7] This is such a central ritual symbol in Islam that a Muslim ruler is encouraged to wage war against a city whose inhabitants do not perform *khitān* to force them back to normative Islamic conduct.[8] Other jurists deem male circumcision as "highly desired" (*mustaḥabb*) only[9]—a qualification which in practice does not result in anything different from *wājib*.

Female circumcision is usually described by the jurists in four alternative ways: (a) *makruma lilnisā'*[10] (act of nobility by the wo-

---

[4] Maḥmūd Shaltūt, "khitān al-unthā", in: *Al-Fatāwā*, 3rd edition, Cairo 1966.

[5] Dr. Muḥammad Al-Hawārī, *Al-Khitān fī Al-Yahūdiyya wAl-Masīḥiyya wAl-Islām*, 1st edition, Cairo 1987, p. 125.

[6] On the connection between violence and love see for example: Abdelwahab Bouhdiba, *Sexuality in Islam*, London 1985, p. 184.

[7] *Majallat Al-Tawḥīd*, Muḥarram 1409, p. 21; Makhlūf, *Al-Fatāwā Al-Islāmiyya*, v. 2, p. 449; *Liwā' Al-Islām*, April 6, 1989, p. 55 (a *fatwā* by Muḥammad 'Abd Allah Al-Khaṭīb); *Majallat Al-Azhar*, February 1981.

[8] Dr. Yūsuf Al-Qirḍāwī, *Fatāwā Mu'āṣira*, 3rd edition, Kuwait 1987, p. 443.

[9] *Al-Nūr*, September 6, 1989, p. 8 (a *fatwā* by Dr. Muṣṭafā 'Amāra).

[10] For the typical medical approach see for example the Shi'ite Ibn Bābawayhi, *Man lā Yaḥḍuruhu Al-Faqīh*, 4th edition, Najf 1957, v. 3, p. 314.

Among the contemporary sources: *Majallat Al-Azhar*, November 1981, p. 315; *Fatāwā 'Abd Al-Ḥālīm Maḥmūd*, Cairo 1986, v. 2, pp. 304-305; Makhlūf, *Fatāwā Shar'iyya waBuḥūth Islāmiyya*, Cairo 1952, v. 2, pp. 208-209; Cairo 1971, v. 1, p. 146; Cairo 1980, v. 2, p. 449; Al-Sha'rāwī, *Al-Fatāwā, Kull mā Yahimm Al-Muslim fī Ḥayātihi waYawmihi waGhaddihi*, Cairo n.d., v. 1, p. 21; Dr. Yūsuf Al-Qirḍāwī,

men), meaning that it adds to the woman's dignity if practiced: it is not considered a sin if it is not performed. This is allegedly the Mālikī legal opinion. (b) *sunna* (good practice, as exemplified by the Prophet), that is, less than obligatory but very strongly encouraged.[11] This is believed to be the Ḥanbalī legal approach. (c) *jā'iz*, permissible, or "neutral" from a Shar'ī point of view, and definitely not obligatory.[12] (d) *wājib* (obligatory for females just as for males). This is allegedly the Shāfi'ī law.[13]

The first two options are the most prevalent. They are also the less definite and more flexible semantically and legally. Options (a) and (b) are those responsible for the legal obscurity in which female circumcision in Islamic law is shrouded.

Sheikh Shaltūt, however, objects to all four options, because no legal text can in fact support any of them.[14] He found no legal justification of any kind to perform female circumcision.

Muslim authors identify the historical origins of circumcision as either ancient Egyptian or pre-Islamic customs. In ancient Egypt circumcision was an act of purification required of anyone who wished to join the temple and the priestly cast.[15] The Egyptian Hagar and Joseph, who lived in Egypt, were those responsible for spreading circumcision, first among the Jews and then among the Muslims.[16]

Fatāwā Mu'āṣira, p. 443; *Majallat Al-Tawḥīd*, Muḥarram 1409, p. 21; Jād Al-Ḥaqq 'Alī Jād Al-Ḥaqq (in a *fatwā* dated January 29, 1981), in: *Al-Fatāwā Al-Islāmiyya*, v. 9, pp. 3119-3125.

11 Sheikh 'Allām Naṣṣār, in: *Al-Fatāwā Al-Islāmiyya*, Cairo 1982, v. 6, pp. 1985-1986 (the *fatwā* is dated June 23, 1951); *Al-Taṣawwuf Al-Islāmī*, August 1979; Makhlūf, see note no. 10; Rashīd Riḍa, *Fatāwā Rashīd Riḍā*, 1st edition, Beirut 1970, v. 1, pp. 245-246 (the *fatwā* is dated 1904).

12 *Majallat Al-Tawḥīd*, Sha'bān 1408, no. 8, p. 20 (a *fatwā* by Sheikh Muḥammad 'Alī 'Abd Al-Raḥīm).

13 *Fatāwā 'Abd Al-Ḥalīm Maḥmūd*, v. 2, pp. 304-305; Makhlūf (note 10 above). According to the Mālikīs, Ḥanbalīs and Ḥanafīs, *khafḍ* is only *makruma lilnisā'*, i.e. *sunna*. According to the Shāfi'īs it is *wājib* to both males and females. See: Dr. Wahba Al-Zuḥaylī, *Al-Fiqh Al-Islāmī wa Adillatuhu*, 3rd edition, Damascus 1989, v.1, pp. 306-307; p. 310.

14 *Al-Fatāwā*, Cairo 1966, pp. 330-334.

15 Al-Sayyid Muḥammad 'Āshūr, *Al-Khitān fī Al-Sharā'i' Al-Samāwiyya wal-Waḍ'iyya*, p. 15; Al-Sha'rāwī, *Al-Fatāwā kull mā Yahimm Al-Muslim fī Ḥayātihi wa Yawmihi waGhaddihi*, p. 21.

16 'Āshūr, ibid., p. 69.

The pre-Islamic Arabs considered the *khitān* as a precaution against dangerous illness. *Khitān* was approved by the Prophet after the pagan custom had already been adapted to Islamic conduct.[17]

The two different possible origins of circumcision, the ancient Egyptian and the pre-Islamic, should not be viewed as contradictory. Olayinka Koso-Thomas, who wrote about female circumcision in Africa (where Muslims are only one of the groups which practice the custom), states that "many authors believe the practice started simultaneously in different parts of the world."[18]

It is immaterial whether female circumcision in Islam originated from ancient Egypt or from pre-Islamic Arabia. What matters is that its roots were definitely non-Islamic. Like other pagan customs, *khitān* had to go through a process of adaptation to Islamic legal norms. The recurrent claim that in performing circumcision Muslims imitate the practice of Abraham and Hagar is only part of this process.

The right age to undergo the procedure is not unanimously agreed by Muslim scholars. Several times are nevertheless suggested for males to be circumcised, while not much mention is made regarding the preferred circumcision age for females. The obscurity around the issue today follows the medieval precedent. On the one hand it is related that the Prophet circumcised his two grandchildren, Ḥasan and Ḥusayn at the age of seven days, thus establishing one model.[19] On the other hand it is often asked if a child should suffer pain at all before he reaches the age of legal responsibility (*taklīf*), which is roughly defined as ten years.[20]

Another fact to consider is that the older the child the more painful circumcision becomes; this could speak for preferring the younger age for circumcision.[21] Abraham appears to be the earliest source of confusion—or flexibility, depending on one's opinion, since he circumcised Isaac at the age of seven days, while he circumcised Ismāʿīl at

---

[17] Dr. Muḥammad Al-Hawārī, *Al-Khitān fī Al-Yahūdiyya wAl-Masīḥiyya wAl-Islām*, p. 86; *Fatāwā Rashīd Riḍā*, v. 1, pp. 245-246.

[18] *The Circumcision of Women: A Strategy for Eradication*, UK 1987, p. 15.

[19] Ibn Al-Ḥājj, *Al-Madkhal*, 1st edition, Cairo 1960, v. 3, pp. 310-311; Ibn Bābawayhī, *Man lā Yaḥḍuruhu Al-Faqīh*, v. 3, p. 314.

[20] Shaltūt, *Al-Fatāwā*, pp. 330-334. Some scholars tend to link the age of *khitān* to the age at which a child may be beaten for neglecting the duty to pray—ten years. They explain that *khitān* is more painful than those beatings. See: Dr. Muḥammad Al-Hawārī (note 17), p. 107.

[21] *Al-Nūr*, November 21, 1990, p. 7.

the age of thirteen years.[22] Other suggested ages for circumcision of males are 40 days or seven years.[23] The duty to circumcise males is completely waived in cases such as when the baby is born circumcised, when he is too weak, or when an elderly man converts to Islam and his infirm health prevents the operation.[24]

There appears to be even more flexibility with regard to the preferred age for female circumcision. Although one opinion suggests an age between seven and nine years,[25] another leaves the age to the discretion of the girl's guardian (*waliyy al-amr*).[26] The latter opinion obviously takes into consideration the individual condition and the physical as well as mental readiness of the girl to withstand so traumatic an operation. Such a consideration should be accredited to the progressive thinking of the *muftī* who gave it.

All legal sources agree that male circumcision involves the excision of the foreskin. But there is no unanimity as to what female circumcision entails.

Of the three kinds of female circumcision known to human civilizations, clitoridectomy, excision and infibulation,[27] Muslim jurists seem to recommend the smallest operation, namely, clitoridectomy.[28] In Arabic it is called *khafḍ* meaning lowering of the clitoris, that is the removal of the foreskin which protects the clitoris. The piece of skin which has to be removed is described as being the size of a stone of a fruit or of a cockscomb.[29]

Khafḍ is based on a tradition in which the Prophet ordered the woman in charge of such operations, sometimes referred to as Umm ʿAṭiyya, "*ashimmī walā tanhakī*" ("lower, but do not completely up-

---

[22] Ibn Qayyim, *Zād Al-Maʿād*, Beirut 1982, v. 2, p. 4; Al-Sayyid Muḥammad ʿĀshūr, *Al-Khitān fī Al-Sharāʾiʿ Al-Samāwiyya*, p. 69.

[23] *Fatāwā ʿAbd Al-Ḥalīm Maḥmūd*, v. 2, pp. 304-305.

[24] Dr. Muḥammad Al-Hawārī (note 17 above), pp. 113-114.

[25] Sheikh ʿAbd Al-Munṣif Maḥmūd, in: *Al-Liwāʾ Al-Islāmī*, February 15, 1990, p. 7.

[26] Jād Al-Ḥaqq ʿAlī Jād Al-Ḥaqq, in: *Al-Fatāwā Al-Islāmiyya*, v. 9, pp. 3119-3125. The *fatwā* is dated January 29, 1981.

[27] Clitoridectomy means the removal of the prepuce of the clitoris; Excision means removal of the prepuce, the clitoris itself and all or part of the labia minora; Infibulation means the removal of all of the above in addition to stitching together the two sides of the vulva leaving a very small orifice for the flow of urine and menstrual discharge. See: Olayinka Koso-Thomas, *The Circumcision of Women*, pp. 16-17.

[28] Ibid.

[29] Dr. Muḥammad Al-Hawārī, *Al-Khitān fī Al-Yahūdiyya wAl-Masīḥiyya wAl-Islām*, p. 102.

root!")[30] or *"ikhfiḍī walā tanhakī!"* with the same meaning.[31] The principle of *khafḍ* is that something *zā'id* (superfluous) must be removed, but without exaggeration. If the superfluous piece is non-existent, nothing is to be removed. There is a popular belief in existence, at least since the fourteenth century, that women in the Orient have a superfluous piece of skin over their clitoris, and this must be removed; in the West women lack it, and therefore no *khafḍ* is required of them.[32] However, philosophical questions such as why did God create people with "superfluous" pieces of skin and others without? If God is responsible for the existence of superfluous organs, why should man remove them? Can wholeness be achieved via mutilation and amputation? Surely God's creation is complete as it is and doesn't need further correction—are not addressed by our sources at all.

The reason for a partial removal only of this piece of skin is that it is better for the woman and more pleasurable for her husband.[33] In other words, having undergone *khafḍ* a woman improves her social status, her husband likes her more and consequently treats her better.

It is overtly stated that female circumcision is intended to control and restrain the female's sexual drive. A circumcised wife is believed to be more faithful to her husband, hence more dignified herself and a source of dignity to him too. The fear of female sexuality, which is responsible for the majority of the Sharʿī laws concerning women (such as their exposure to the public eye, their rebelliousness, their clothing, granting them permission to work outside the home etc.) is also responsible for advocating female circumcision.

In this regard it is often mentioned that an uncircumcised wife might fall into *zinā* (adultery), for the simple reason that her husband will never succeed in satisfying her sexual needs.[34] For the virgin woman and the girl at puberty, being uncircumcised might lead to other

---

[30] Dr. Yūsuf Al-Qirḍāwī, *Fatāwā Muʿāṣira*, p. 443.

[31] Sheikh ʿAbd Al-Munṣif Maḥmūd, in: *Al-Liwā' Al-Islāmī*, February 15, 1990, p. 7; *Al-Taṣawwuf Al-Islāmī*, August 1979; *Majallat Al-Azhar*, February 1981.

[32] Al-Shaʿrāwī, *Al-Fatāwā Kull mā Yahimm Al-Muslim fī Ḥayātihi waYawmihi waGhaddihi*, v. 1, p. 21; Ḥasanayn Muḥammad Makhlūf, *Fatāwā Sharʿiyya waBuḥūth Islāmiyya*, v. 2, pp. 208-209; Ibn Al-Ḥājj, *Al-Madkhal*, v. 3, pp. 310-311.

[33] Dr. Yūsuf Al-Qirḍāwī (note 30); *Fatāwā ʿAbd Al-Ḥalīm Maḥmūd*, v. 2, pp. 304-305.

[34] Dr. Muḥammad Al-Hawārī, *Al-Khitān fī Al-Yahūdiyya wAl-Masīḥiyya wAl-Islām*, p. 103.

problems, among them promiscuity, which is alluded to but not specified.[35]

Circumcision is lauded as a protective measure against sexual temptations for women at all ages, something which has become indispensable in present-day crowded neighborhoods, and in the face of the modern tempting situations awaiting a girl. Circumcision is a barrier to *inḥirāf* and *fasād* (perversion and unchastity).[36]

More extreme accounts state that where circumcision is not performed on women they tend to practice lesbian relationships,[37] (*siḥāq*) which are as condemned in Islamic law as male homosexual relationships (*liwāṭ*) are.[38] We may deduce from this that lesbianism is at least partially understood by religious scholars as the outcome of sexual lust which is never satisfied.

On the other hand, a woman whose circumcision was "exaggerated" or "overdone" might lose all sexual interest in her husband, which is not only an undesirable outcome for the man[39] but also defeats the purpose for which the sexual organs were created. As a result of this "exaggeration" some men are driven to use sexual stimulants. Some women engage in forbidden acts despite their being circumcised.[40] Shaltūt, in a very courageous stand, concludes that there is no medical, ethical or Shar'ī support for female circumcision, and that female chastity is dependent only on education and supervision. No physical measures can guarantee chastity.[41] Several other scholars also dared to assert that if *khafḍ* is not practiced, no sin was committed.[42]

Even the advantages so often associated with female circumcision cannot hide the fact that *khitān* may cause health problems to the woman such as the inability to enjoy natural sexual relations, mental disorders, physical damage, primarily hemorrhage and injury to the uri-

---

35 *Al-Nūr*, November 21, 1990, p. 7.

36 Jād Al-Ḥaqq 'Alī Jād Al-Ḥaqq, in: *Al-Fatāwā Al-Islāmiyya*, v. 9, pp. 3119-3125 (the *fatwā* is dated January 29, 1981).

37 Sheikh 'Abd Al-Munṣif Maḥmūd, in: *Al-Liwā' Al-Islāmī*, February 15, 1990, p. 7; *Al-Umma Al-Islāmiyya*, December 1985, p. 9.

38 On the prohibition of lesbian relations, see for example: Ibn Al-Jawzī *Kitāb Aḥkām Al-Nisā'*, 1st edition, Beirut 1988, pp. 118-119.

39 Dr. Muḥammad Al-Hawārī, p. 103.

40 Maḥmūd Shaltūt, *Al-Fatāwā*, pp. 330-334.

41 Ibid.

42 *Al-Nūr*, July 10, 1991, p. 7; Makhlūf, *Fatāwā Shar'iyya waBuḥūth Islāmiyya*, v. 1, p. 146.

nary system.[43] The health hazards acknowledged by Muslim scholars are few compared with those found empirically and medically. Koso-Thomas, for example, groups the hazards as follows:

a. immediate (including pain, hemorrhage, shock, acute urinary retention, urinary infection, blood poisoning, fever, tetanus, death and fractured clavicle);
b. intermediate (including delay in wound healing, pelvic infection, cysts and abscesses, keloid scar, painful intercourse);
c. late complications (including closure of the vaginal opening by the scar tissue, infertility, recurrent urinary tract infection, difficulty in urinating, stone formation, hypersenstivity and incontinence and fissure);
d. in consummation (difficulty in penetration, fear of the sex act, failure of the circumcision scar to dilate);
e. at delivery (prolonged and obstructed labor, unnecessary Caesarian section, other gynecological consequences, stillbirth, mentally handicapped children, etc.);
f. postnatal complications (miscarriages, descent of uterus into the vagina);
g. sexual problems (lack of orgasm, frigidity, anxiety, depression, temporary impotence and frustration over long-lasting inability to consummate marriage).[44]

In defense of female circumcision it is claimed that the damages which occur do so only when circumcision is performed by inexperienced people.[45] Another claim is that doctors who condemn circumcision as being hazardous for females do so only to displace the midwives, who have performed most circumcisions until today. Doctors wish to entrust the operation solely to surgeons, whom they believe will perform it with greater safety and success.[46]

Whether these two claims are justified or not, they both aim to attribute any harm that results from circumcision to faults in procedure rather than the nature of the operation itself. One major argument for

---

[43] Al-Sayyid Muḥammad ʿĀshūr, *Al-Khitān fī Al-Sharāʾiʿ Al-Samāwiyya wal-Waḍʿiyya*, p. 38.
[44] Olayinka Koso-Thomas, *The Circumcision of Women*, pp. 25-28.
[45] *Al-Nūr*, November 21, 1990, p. 7.
[46] Sheikh ʿAllām Naṣṣār, in: *Al-Fatāwā Al-Islāmiyya*, v. 6, 1982, pp. 1985-1986 (the *fatwā* is dated June 23, 1951).

this is that the Supreme Legislator, who is supposedly responsible for initiating the practice of female circumcision, would never have ordered a hazardous step to be taken. Only shortcomings in human understanding prevent us from discovering the full wisdom behind female circumcision or permit the view that it may be a medical hazard. In time this wisdom will be better understood, as is already the case with other decrees of God, and obviously the alleged perilousness of the operation will vanish.

Despite the health problems which vary in their degree of severity, but which all circumcised women experience, the practice is geographically widespread. A moderate *khafḍ* is practiced in Chad. About 85 percent of the Sudanese and Somali women undergo *khafḍ*. The Somali women even endure a *khafḍ mubālagh* (extended circumcision), which is medically equal to excision, if not to infibulation. In North Africa, the domain of the Mālikī school of law, *khafḍ* does not take place. This is true for Tunisia, Algeria and Morocco. The Shiʿites of Iraq and the Kurds do not practice *khafḍ* either. In Egypt *khafḍ* was made formally illegal, so it has become restricted predominately to Upper Egypt where a Sudanese influence maybe suspected.[47] *Khafḍ* is apparently not practiced in "the cradle and seat of Islam", for example, Saudi Arabia, the United Arab Emirates, South Yemen, Bahrain and Oman. But it is common among Muslim groups in the Philippines, Malaysia, Pakistan and Indonesia.[48]

The general picture of the geographical distribution of *khafḍ* shows that where Islam has been kept as free as possible from local and pagan influences, *khafḍ* remained prohibited or minimized in accordance with the teachings of the Hadith. But remote from the "cradle of Islam," on the west coast of Africa and in the Far East, *khafḍ* managed to survive. This might suggest that it is foreign customs, not taught by Islamic law, that helped preserve and spread the practice. Wherever Islam is untainted by primitive and pre-Islamic superstitions *khafḍ* is eschewed. The ethics of *khafḍ* when it is practised are in agreement with the general spirit of Islamic law.

Nevertheless, it is not surprising that several Muslim doctors have refused recently to perform circumcisions on girls, either by simply

---

[47] Dr. Muḥammad Al-Hawārī, *Al-Khitān fī Al-Yahūdiyya wAl-Masīḥiyya wAl-Islām*, pp. 141-150. Olayinka Koso-Thomas, *The Circumcision of Women*, p. 17, supports this information.

[48] Ibid.

stating that it is forbidden by religion[49] or by explaining that it is harmful to the girl's body and soul.[50]

We learn of these physicians' attitudes only when the rejected family inquires of the *muftī* if the doctor's approach is right according to religion. There may be many more cases of rejection that are not so openly discussed. The rejected family would anyhow easily find someone else to perform the operation, whether a doctor or not.

Of the various issues of medical ethics we have treated so far, *khafḍ* seems to be the only one in which doctors are those who tend to evade a medical procedure while the legal scholars tolerate it or remain silent. In other issues the doctors were eager to help the patient attain his/her medical goal, sometimes even at the price of breaching a religious dogma.

The reason for this should be sought in the inhuman and violent treatment inflicted on girls during circumcision. It is, after all, the doctors who encounter the young girls' mutilated bodies when circumcision in the traditional form fails. This is enough to provoke them into becoming the leading opponents of the custom. Feminists, in their turn, eagerly use medical descriptions of failed circumcisions in their campaign against what they call "the male oppression of females".

---

49 *Al-Nūr*, November 21, 1990, p. 7.

50 *Al-Fatāwā Al-Islāmiyya*, v. 9, pp. 3119-3125 (a *fatwā* by Jād Al-Ḥaqq 'Alī Jād Al-Ḥaqq dated January 29, 1981).

CHAPTER TEN

EUTHANASIA—MERCY KILLING

Quite often in recent years Western courts have had to decide if the life of a terminally ill person could be ended via disconnecting the machines which kept the patient artificially alive (do-not-resuscitate order, DNR), or if the patient was to be allowed to stop taking medicine and nutrition before his/her brain was dead, in order not to prolong his/her life and suffering.

The ethical dilemmas associated with euthanasia are relatively new, because "until the last fifty years nothing more than rudimentary supportive care could be offered to terminal patients, and, therefore, no ethical dilemmas were created."[1]

In the Western world euthanasia can be approved in response to the patient's own request, or if before his/her health deteriorated the person signed an authorization (sometimes termed "living will") to disconnect life-sustaining machines once the illness worsened to loss of control over the faculties or irreversible coma. About ten million Americans are believed to have made a living will by 1988 and their rights were protected by about three-quarters of the states.[2] But the living will still cannot solve most ethical problems, because seldom does the will foresee the actual medical condition as it develops, when the decision about its fulfilment comes. Judicial intervention is then required.

Sometimes the family of the sick person request euthanasia to preserve the patient's dignity and end the pain, if the patient is comatose for a long period or suffers intolerable pain. If the doctors themselves realize that the patient's condition is beyond cure and that his/her situation is unbearable to the patient, and to the supportive relatives, if there are any, they might suggest euthanasia; or they more likely may bring about death by not trying further medical treatments. The patient is thus left to die passively.

---

[1] Henry A. Shenkin, *Medical Ethics: Evolution, Rights and the Physician*, The Netherlands 1991, p. 354.

[2] Ibid., p. 363.

A more drastic means of euthanasia is the lethal injection, in which case doctors actively participate in causing death. Active euthanasia is illegal in all countries, but its practice is widespread in The Netherlands.[3]

It was correctly argued that although at first sight the difference between active and passive euthanasia seems enormous—the difference between "causing someone's death" and "letting someone die," this difference may be valid only legally. "Fixing the cause of death may be very important from a legal point of view for it may determine whether criminal charges are brought against the doctor." But morally, even "letting somebody die" is a premeditated step, just as "causing somebody's death", so that "no action" by the doctor is not a valid claim. Another ethical dilemma which derives from the foregoing is if letting someone die slowly by withholding nutrition, medicine and resuscitation is not prolonging the pain, while the lethal injection, often viewed as a cruel measure, ends pain much faster, and in fact brings about exactly the same result.[4]

Modern Islamic *fatāwā* do not bother to elaborate on the means through which mercy killing can be executed. These are naturally numerous. Muslim jurists rather view all forms of euthanasia as murder.[5]

Since in Islamic theology the body is not considered to be owned by anyone, no one is free to do with it as he/she wishes, still less to kill it. This is why suicide is forbidden in Islamic law, and it is even forbidden to pray for death to come. God alone may decide on the duration of a life or when it will be ended.

Therefore, since medieval times, Islamic law has spoken of death in fatalistic terms: when death occurs it should be bravely borne with no complaint, no protest and no doubts. Also, when an incurable disease continues for a long period, it should be viewed as an expression of God's will. The patient must then remember that only few chosen people are selected by God to undergo the test of suffering. Consolation should be sought in the knowledge that prophets, jurists and righteous people all eventually die. The soul, however, lives on, and

---

[3] Ibid., p. 379.

[4] James Rachels, "Active and Passive Euthanasia", in: Tom L. Beauchamp and LeRoy Walters (eds.), *Contemporary Issues in Bioethics*, 3rd edition, USA 1989, pp. 245-248.

[5] Jalaluddin Umri, "Suicide or termination of life", translated by S.A.H. Rizvi, *Islam and Comparative Law Quarterly*, 7, 1987, pp. 136-144.

the soul of a believer finally reaches its ultimate rest in Paradise *Ṣabr* (perseverance against pain and agony, self-restraint) is one of the highest virtues a believer may take pride in.[6]

On the other hand, the inability to face disease or death with *ṣabr* is explained as a result of Iblīs's successful attempt to spread despair and doubt as to the existence of Allah's mercy, and to foretell that an even more unbearable pain and torture are still to come.[7]

The medieval sources report that cases of mercy killing were more often performed by a person upon himself than by others. These were mainly intended to save one from intolerable pain. The medieval examples speak of men who were wounded in battle and were either bleeding to death or could no longer stand the pain of their injury, so they chose to terminate the ordeal in an artificial manner. One person stabbed himself to death with his own dagger,[8] another with one of his arrows.[9]

In Islamic law the punishment for killing oneself to escape suffering is that in Hell the suicide will have to endure suffering caused by the same instrument or means which he used on earth to end his life (a sword, an iron bar, poison or falling off a cliff). Needless to say, he will never reach Paradise and no prayers will be offered over his dead body. He will be denied the respect due to any Muslim who dies. Even a person who assisted in the killing of a believer even with a single word can expect none of God's mercies.[10]

Women, who were excluded from the discussion of mercy killing in medieval sources, are nowadays equal participants to men on the issue of euthanasia, both as recipients and as those who bring it about for others.

It is interesting that Islamic law does recognize as legitimate one's desire to die because of an unbearable religious situation or in order to defend one's religion. Bankruptcy and physical pain, however, do not justify one's wish to die.[11]

---

[6] Ibn Al-Jawzī (d. 1201), *Al-Thabāt ʿinda Al-Mamāt*, Beirut 1986, pp. 47, 50, 71, 72, 78.

[7] Ibid., p. 57.

[8] Shams Al-Dīn Al-Dhahabī (d. 1348), *Kitāb Al-Kabā'ir*, Mecca 1356H, pp. 134-135.

[9] Ibn Ḥajar Al-Haythamī (d. 1567), *Al-Zawājir ʿan Iqtirāf al-Kabā'ir*, Cairo 1390H, v. 2, pp. 96-97.

[10] Ibid.

[11] Ibn Ḥazm (d. 1063), *Al-Muḥallā*, Cairo 1347-1352H, v. 5, p. 167.

Maryam, ʿĪsā's mother, is presented as a justified case of wishing to die for religious reasons: she did not want the community to defame her moral-religious behavior, after having borne a fatherless child. By her wish to die she hoped to save her community members from the sins of accusing her of adultery and lying.[12]

It is safe to conclude, therefore, that what are held in Islamic law to be legitimate reasons for killing a person have *no connection to medicine* whatsoever. Among these are apostasy and criminal offenses such as adultery and robbery, to mention only a few.

Aside from that, life is believed never to be pain-free. If whoever suffered pain were allowed to be killed, elderly people and those no longer beneficial to society would have easily been exterminated.[13] This is of course unthinkable in any progressive humane society, and especially in Islam where the Qur'an mentions so often that the needy and destitute, the poor and the sick should never be deserted.

The mercy killing of a terminally sick patient is forbidden in Islamic law because it ignores Allah's ability to perform miracles, and because it interferes with Allah's exclusive control over life and death. In this regard it is recalled that even very sick patients sometimes recover. It is reported in this context that once in Berlin a patient believed to be dead recovered at the gravesite; recovery of sick people, who are not yet dead, is even more likely to occur.[14]

In contemporary cases of mercy killing, the medical staff is sometimes asked to terminate life, after the proper legal authorization has been obtained. But Islamic law holds the doctor and the nurse responsible for maintaining the process of life, not of dying. When a doctor terminates life, it is as if medicine is utilized for the opposite purpose for which it was created by God.[15] It is an offense against the Lord.

Anyone who commits suicide ignores his/her obligations toward his/her relatives. On the other hand, when suicide is meant to release a patient from a malignant and incurable disease, the patient may claim

---

[12] Shams Al-Dīn Al-Qurṭubī (d. 1273), *Al-Tadhkira*, Cairo 1980, p. 13.

[13] First International conference on Islamic Medicine, *Islamic Code of Medical Ethics*, Kuwait, January 1981, pp. 64-65.

[14] Dr. Muḥammad Rajab Al-Bayūmī, "qatl al-marīḍ al-may'ūs minhu", in: *Majallat Al-Azhar*, January-February 1986, pp. 674-678; *Al-Liwā' Al-Islāmī*, February 8, 1990, p. 7.

[15] *Islamic Code of Medical Ethics*, p. 68; Jalaluddin Umri, "Suicide or termination of life."

he/she wished to free relatives of the burden of tending to a bedridden person.[16]

Because of the financial interest which relatives may draw from the death of a next-of-kin, Islamic law decreed that a murderer never inherits. According to the Ḥanafis and Shāfiʿis, even an unintentional killer is not eligible for any part of the bequest.[17] All this is intended to remove even the slightest suspicion that A killed B for the sake of hastening A's enjoyment of B's bequest.

Muslims claim that what made euthanasia acceptable in the West is the disintegration of the family unit. Since loyalty and cohesion within the family no longer exists, there is no incentive to share pain with another. Euthanasia is a solution for those who wish to disclaim all connections with the bedridden patient.[18]

Because of the perceptions of Islamic law (a) that Allah alone decides on life and death, and (b) that the world is a continuous testing ground for mankind, the killing of a terminally ill person is equivalent to murder, on which Islamic law is very clear. According to Ibn Ḥanbal and Mālik, even a person A who forces another B to kill a third is worthy of *qiṣāṣ* (vengeance).[19] In other words, indirect participation in killing is equated with killing, at least with regard to the due punishment. If this principle is stretched somewhat, it means that anyone who was ever consulted and opined in favor of euthanasia, all the more the doctor who disconnected the life-sustaining machine and the relative who signed the authorizing papers, are guilty of the same crime— murder.[20]

---

[16] Jalaluddin Umri, "Suicide or termination of life."

[17] The four schools of law are unanimous that killing prohibits inheriting, but they are divided about the type of killing that validates the prohibition. Abū Ḥanīfa refers to intentional as well as unintentional killing; Mālik refers only to intentional killing. Shāfiʿī considers any type of killing as prohibiting inheritance, even out of negligence. Ibn Ḥanbal referred to any type of killing which entails either a *qiṣāṣ* or a *diya* (blood money) or a *kafāra* (compensation) as prohibiting inheritance. See: Dr. Wahba Al-Zuḥaylī, *Al-Fiqh Al-Islami wa'Adillatuh*, 3rd edition, Damascus 1989, v. 8, pp. 260-262.

[18] Jalaluddin Umri, "Suicide or termination of life."

[19] Mālikīs, Shāfiʿīs and Ḥanbalīs request *qiṣāṣ* for both A and B, while Abū Ḥanīfa and Muḥammad Al-Shaybānī request *qiṣāṣ* only for A, not for B, because B is just instrumental to A, not the true killer. See: Dr. Wahbah Al-Zuhayly, *Al-Fiqh Al-Islami, wa'Adillatuh*, v. 6, p. 241.

[20] Sheikh Muḥammad ʿAbd Allah Al-Khaṭīb, in: *Liwāʾ Al-Islām*, September 1, 1989, p. 57.

The negative Islamic ethical attitude toward euthanasia emerges from all the foregoing. No exceptions to the rule have ever been made. For the hopelessly sick Muslim, *ṣabr*, as a strong characteristic of total belief in God's power, is the only recourse available to endure suffering. He/she may also be consoled with the hope that suffering has a purifying impact on the soul and on its preparation for the eternal rest in Paradise. For these theological considerations, other ethical discussions pertaining to euthanasia in the Western world, have no place in the ethical thinking of Muslims. These questions are whether the high costs of maintaining the dying should not be substituted by better health services for those who have a chance of recovering; and whether non-terminal patients whose quality of life has no prospect of improving, such as severely deformed newborn babies and patients in a vegetative state, should also be included in the "terminally ill" category.

CHAPTER ELEVEN

AIDS

One of the most recent medical issues which Islamic law has to address is AIDS. The illness, which was first made public in 1979, has been mentioned in Muslim's ethical literature since about 1985.

It took Muslims (as well as others) some five years to realize the dimension of the illness and consequently to admit that it is not only a problem pertaining to European and American homosexuals, as was so convenient to believe when AIDS first appeared. Muslims, even when not directly afflicted by the disease, had at least to be warned against it.

Islamic sources sometimes provide medical information as to the ways by which the AIDS virus is transmitted, and that women are less likely to contract the disease than men. They also conclude that the safest way to escape AIDS nowadays is total abstention from sex.[1] Symptoms of the disease and its similarity to cancer are mentioned as well.[2] But this is not the complete portrayal of AIDS in modern *fatāwā*.

Most of the *fatāwā* on AIDS are eager to prove that the illness would not have existed had people adopted the Islamic life-style. In other words, the Islamic religion, according to the *fatāwā* can function as the best barrier to AIDS. The apologetic aspect is given priority over the curative and practical aspects.

The reason for the spread of AIDS is therefore the sexual promiscuity prevalent in Europe and America.[3] Other times, the reason is claimed to be perverted sexual contacts.[4] In a more detailed *fatwā*, homosexual relations, adultery and contaminated syringes used by

---

[1] "raghma ṣu'ūbat al-iṣāba bil-AIDS fa'innahu ghayr qābil lil-shifā'", in: *Al-I'tiṣām*, August 1987, pp. 20-21. The article actually quotes Margaret A. Mitchell, the head of the AIDS program at the University of Miami.

[2] "al-AIDS wabā' al-fāḥisha ilā ayna?", in: *Majallat Al-Azhar*, June 1987, pp. 1399-1402 (Dr. Wāṣif 'Abd Al-Ḥalīm 'Abd Allah).

[3] "al-AIDS wadawr al-qawānīn al-islāmiyya fī al-wiqāya minhu", in: *Al-I'tiṣām*, November-December 1985, pp. 18-21; *Majallat Al-Azhar*, June 1987, pp. 1399-1402.

[4] "hadhā huwa 'iqāb Allah lil munḥarifīn", in: *Al-I'tiṣām*, December 1986-January 1987, p. 18.

drug addicts are depicted as means of transmitting the disease.[5] There is no mention in the *fatwās* of the possibility of contacting the disease via blood transfusions in a manner which is remote from perversion and for which the patient himself/herself bears no responsibility whatsoever.

The victims of the illness are those who practice perverted sex[6] or even anyone who maintains sexual relations with anyone other than his lawful wife.[7]

While perverted sex refers to *liwāṭ* (male homosexuality, lesbianism, sex with animals, etc.) the other group of victims is those who perform *zinā* (adultery) in the widest sense of the term as used in the spoken language, that is, sex outside a marital framework. This *zinā* differs from the Sharʿī definition of zinā which is reserved for sexual intercourse between two people not married to each other but of whom one at least is married.

Both *liwāṭ* and *zinā* are punishable by death in Islamic law, to highlight its intolerance toward crimes held to be destructive of stable family life, and hence to Islamic society at large.

The cure which Islamic law offers against AIDS is to encourage youth to marry, and so to satisfy sexual needs within the marital unit. On the other had, there is a strong prohibition against practicing *zinā, liwāṭ* and any form of perverted sex (*shudhūdh*).[8] It is of course always recommended to turn back to Allah and behave according to His Sharīʿa.[9]

Finally, the Qur'an is evoked regarding AIDS too, to prove that Allah foresaw all abominations (*fawāḥish*) and warned against them already in 7,33: "Say: May Lord forbiddeth only indecencies, such of them as are apparent and such as are within, and sin and wrongful oppression..."[10]

The inevitable conclusion that an intelligent Muslim must draw from all the above-mentioned arguments, is that devotion to Allah leads to immunity from AIDS.

Questions such as the financing and location of health care for AIDS patients; should the latter pursue normal family and work life

[5] *Majallat Al-Azhar*, June 1987, pp. 1399-1402.
[6] *Al-Iʿtiṣām*, November-December 1985.
[7] *Al-Iʿtiṣām*, December 1986-January 1987.
[8] *Al-Iʿtiṣām*, November-December 1986.
[9] *Al-Iʿtiṣām*, December 1986-January 1987.
[10] M.M. Pickthall, *The Meaning of the Glorious Koran*, London and USA n.d.

while they are sick; may a physician who knows he/she is carrying the virus treat patients without informing them of his/her condition, etc. None of these is discussed in contemporary *fatāwā* at all. The *muftīs* seem to ignore the situation of those already afflicted with the disease, and prefer to concentrate on charging them with leading immoral lives and warning others against the desertion of the Path of Allah.

CHAPTER TWELVE

MISCELLANY

This chapter includes translations and annotations of recently issued *fatāwā*, the topics of which are related to medical ethics. They are not however discussed in the previous chapters of the book because most of these *fatāwā* have been collected without a match or with only one counterpart as far as the subject is concerned, and are therefore presented to the reader in their full translation, not in summary. While the interest which is obviously involved with unique *fatwā*s and the legal opinions which they convey is immense, one must be careful not to jump to general conclusions vis a vis the respective medical ethics based on little legal evidence. Some of these *fatwā*s, especially the one which discusses the legitimacy of banks of mothers' milk, and the one which discusses the legitimacy of freezing a man's seed in order to use it at some point after his death, are what might be called "revolutionary" or "pioneering" and should be for the time being assessed as representing the *muftī* who issued them only, not as a publicly accepted rule. This does not mean that at a later stage, one *muftī*'s opinion will not become the accepted rule, which is after all the strength of the legal tool of the *fatwā*.

The full translation of the following *fatwā*s could also be beneficial for readers who are not well acquainted with the legal and literacy forms of the *fatwā*.

Ten subjects have been selected to be covered by this chapter.

Subject I deals with healing, and is discussed on the one hand by a *fatwā* of ʿAbd Al-Ḥalīm Maḥmūd who addresses the general question of whether medicine plays any role at all when God is the Supreme Healer?! Consequently, is it worthwhile for humans to strive to find the cure which ultimately is in the hands of Allah? On the other hand, there is a *fatwā* by Sheik ʿAṭiyya Ṣaqr which emphasizes the importance of maintaining good mental and physical health as encouraged in both the Qur'an and Hadith. This last *fatwā*, which is concerned with the roles and liability of various healers and doctors in addition to a particular case of sex change surgery (already mentioned in Chapter

5), deposits much of the healing responsibilities in the hands of humans. Seeking cure is an obligation upon mankind as much as the prevention of diseases. The fact that Allah is the ultimate Healer and that He decides about life and death, sickness and health, does not withhold from the personal and communal duties to better life, ease death and hasten cure for the diseases whenever available.

Subject II discusses the impact of drinking wine on the human body. The approach of Sheikh Shaltūt, the *muftī*, is typical to many medical ethics in that he aims to show that the prohibition of wine in Islamic law coincides with recent medical arguments against wine drinking and its hazards. It is not surprising that recent discoveries showing that drinking alcohol moderately on a daily basis is good for the heart (as is already mentioned in medical textbooks such as Harrison's *Principles of Internal Medicine*, 10th edition, 1983, p. 1472) are ignored by Muslim scholars.

Subject III includes a justification of the prohibition of using drugs or consuming pork-meat from both a religious and a medical point of view. Similarly to the *fatwā* on wine drinking, this *fatwā* also aims at proving the logic behind the Islamic laws and their attentiveness to the medical welfare of Muslims. This *fatwā* lists an unusually long account of the diseases that pork-eaters may encounter—possibly for the purpose of dressing the Qur'anic prohibition with scientific facts, thus satisfying the modern skeptical Muslim who is likely today to meet non-Muslims who eat pork-meat and be dragged into a debate over its nutritious value.

Subject IV tackles the ambivalence of Islamic law toward smoking cigarettes, for and against permitting it, through two *fatwā*s: one by Shaltūt and the other by Maḥmūd. These two *fatwā*s represent the modern legal treatment of issues which classical legal sources did not speak of, for the simple reason that the dilemma arose only after the classical period of legislation in Islam (8th-9th centuries). Tobacco was introduced into the Islamic world much later. The hazards of smoking, which both *muftī*s recognize, render smoking close to the previously forbidden consumption of wine, drugs and unclean meats. Yet the medical aspect of smoking is not the only one considered. Social, economic and educational aspects are mentioned too. Maḥmūd is more liberal in that he stipulated the prohibition/permission on the individual circumstances of the smoker. Shaltūt is more decisive in prohibiting smoking, especially since he believes that governments bear responsibility in protecting their youth.

Subject V deals with the recently established banks of mothers' milk. Are they legitimate from an Islamic point of view?

These banks have developed thanks to advancements in refrigeration and transportation. The subject was evoked also because of the importance which modern medicine has rediscovered in mother's milk and its advantages for the development of healthy babies. The establishment of banks of milk poses a religious obstacle to Muslims whose religious law attributes genealogical hereditary powers to milk almost as strong as those associated with blood. Hence, all children who suckle the milk of the same woman over a fixed measurement, are perceived by law as brothers and sisters. An immediate result is that they may not marry one another. Banks of milk, therefore, can be viewed as the enemies of solid social foundations which Islamic law so zealously protects. Since the milk donation is disconnected from its natural source, cases of incest may occur. Thus banks of milk place science and social equilibrium at loggerheads.

Immediately connected to the above is the question as to whether a woman should be forced to breast-feed a child, when the other possible option is hiring a wetnurse. (No mention has been made in the *fatwā* of the chemical formula—artificial baby's nutrition—as an alternative to mother's milk, or of animals' milk for the same purpose. Again, Islamic law, which obligates the mother to breast-feed only in few cases, is shown to be attentive to the psychological and nutritional advantages of breast-feeding for the baby, since the law recommends breast-feeding even when not required.

Subject VI deals with the logic behind the Islamic instruction to avoid sexual intercourse with a menstruating woman. On the one hand it is stressed that the Islamic instruction is more liberal than the Jewish one, and indirectly it is thus claimed not to be as strict as it appears from first impression. On the other hand the wisdom of keeping sexually away from the menstruating woman is shown to be in agreement with medical knowledge—the susceptibility of the female body to illnesses during the menstrual period; Islamic law and medicine are supportive of one another in this case, and both care for the welfare of man.

Subject VII is a debate over an exceptional case of a woman who requested legal permission to freeze her husband's sperm in order to be impregnated with it after his death. Sheikh Al-Mushidd sides with the liberal approach and permits it, provided that it is verified that the sperm is indeed her husband's, hence adultery will not be performed.

Shalabī, however, disagrees with Sheikh Al-Mushidd and raises several additional ethical dilemma, which although unforeseen at the moment, might result from such a permission at a later stage.

The *fatwā* tackles one extreme case of artificial insemination. It contains all the ethical dilemma of artificial insemination as we have widely discussed (see Chapter 3), in addition to those related to the unusual date of insemination, and the social status of the woman at that date. Technically, modern medicine has no difficulty in performing such an insemination. But the achievements of medicine have not alleviated all the ethical problems. This *fatwā* echoes internal disputes among Muslim scholars over the legitimacy of a medical technique which is already in use in the West. The feasibility of the technique is not in question. What is questionable is whether Muslims are allowed to utilize it for their own good as much as non-Muslims.

Subject VIII displays two *fatwā*s on masturbation and whether it is legitimate from a sharʿī point of view. Surprisingly enough, the often more balanced Sheikh Maḥmūd resorts to folkloristic claims that masturbation could lead to many physical ailments, while as the fundamentalist Al-Shaʿrāwī refutes any connection between masturbation and developing ailments. This does not stop both *muftī*s from offering the same cure for preventing this negative phenomenon: marriage, prayer, fast and sports.

Subject IX discusses epilepsy as representative of mental and physical disorders that may disrupt the normal marital life of a couple. The main debate runs over defects which are discovered in one of the spouses only after the consummation of the marriage, and whether they justify annulment of marriage or legal separation with their respective implications, based on the assumption that the contract had either not been valid from the beginning, or had been breached by the concealment of a pre-existing handicap.

The *fatwā* by Jād Al-Ḥaqq clearly demonstrates that there is a widely accepted view that being of good health at the time of marriage is a necessary condition for both spouses, (even when not overtly stipulated), in order to maintain the validity of the marriage contract (unless it is known otherwise and agreed upon in advance). In other words, being of good health or bad health can respectively either fortify or ruin the legitimate grounds of the social/legal bond of marriage.

Curative medicine is essential therefore to enable the transition from bad health to good health. If and when it is effective, curative medicine can restore security to the spouses, the children and the wider family too.

Preventive medicine is even more preferable, since it saves all parties involved the pains of uncertainty and instability (the physical pains, though not mentioned, are obviously avoided too). The real question at stake seems to be whether consummation of marriage voids all pre-marital factors, or not. If it does, as Jād Al-Ḥaqq suggests, then the status of woman after marriage is elevated as no reference to her past misfortunes can be made in an attempt to annul the marriage. If divorce is nevertheless desired by the husband, the wife is entitled to all the *Sharʿī* rights of a divorcee.

Subject X touches upon the preventive aspect in dental care—the *siwāk.* Dental care as a whole is seldom discussed among medical ethics.

In the *fatwā* taken from the fundamentalist newspaper *Al-Iʿtiṣām*, the pure dental element is only an instrument to prove that Islamic law, with its promotion of using the *siwāk* since medieval times, places Islamic civilization ahead of other civilizations which came to recognize the advantages of the toothbrush only in recent generations.

At the same time, in this *fatwā* Muslims themselves are attacked for not realizing that Islamic law contains so many good ideas. The result is that Islamic ideas have first to be acknowledged and appreciated abroad, by non-Muslims, before Muslims recognize the merits of their laws and religion. In the meantime the West treats those ideas as their own and Muslims, because of futile internal struggles, have later to import their original ideas from others, and at a much higher price.

Nevertheless, the *siwāk* is still the sole channel through which dental ethics are discussed, at least as far as my sources have attested.

I. About Healing

Fatāwa ʿAbd Al-Ḥalīm Maḥmūd
2nd edition, Cairo n.d., v. 2, p. 323

Question: "Some people avoid medical treatment and going to the doctor, saying that the only healer is Allah. What is the religious position on this?"

Answer: According to Islamic belief, God may He be praised and exalted is the Healer. Allah says in the words of Ibrāhīm "And when I sicken, then He healeth me" (Qur'an 26, 80) and there is no dispute about it.

However, healing does not differ from other issues, for Allah created their means and ordered us to use them. The laws of the world which God created are such that each result has its cause. Healing is therefore a result which has a cause. This is why the Messenger of Allah said, as quoted by Al-Tirmidhī:[1] "Oh servants of Allah, seek the cure, because Allah did not create a disease without creating its cure, except for one disease. The Messenger of God was asked: what is it? He said: senility. Muslim[2] relates on the authority of the Messenger of God who said "each disease has its cure, and if the cure matches the disease, the person recovers with God's permission."

The Messenger of God emphasizes the law of cause and effect and says overtly: "Allah did not create a disease without a cure, He taught it to whoever He taught, and did not teach it to whoever He decided except for the toxic which is death."

Minbar Al-Islām
October 1988, pp. 132-134
Sheikh ʿAṭiyya Ṣaqr

Medical activities in the shade of Sharʿī laws and ethics

1. Human beings like all other creatures in this life are exposed to health and sickness, right and wrong. Sickness occurs when the bodily faculties are damaged because of an internal or an external reason.
2. There is no doubt that health is preferable to sickness and right is better than wrong. To be healthy, like to be right, is desired by the average person, it is acceptable to logic and supported by the religions.
3. Islam wishes that the Muslim be of a healthy body, strong build, of sound mind and of moral behavior. In the Hadith it is asserted "A powerful believer is preferred and better liked by Allah than a

---

[1] Ibn Qayyim Al-Jawziyya, *Zād Al-Maʿād fī Hudā Khayr Al-ʿIbād*, Beirut 1982, v. 3 p. 66. This hadith is attributed also to Aḥmad b. Ḥanbal, Al-Bukhārī and Muslim.

[2] *Zād al-Maʿād*, v. 3, pp. 66-67. The fact that the proper medicine is found to a particular disease is a sign of God's good will.

weak believer."[3] This strength relies on two issues: supplying the body with all that strengthens it, and protecting the body against all that harms or weakens it. The first is based on foods, beverages and their derivatives. The second is based on prevention of diseases and on treating diseases that have already occurred.

4. In the realm of strength of body and soul Allah has permitted all the good things. Many verses in the Qur'an support this. Among them: "Eat of that which is lawful and wholesome in the earth" (2,168) "Say, who hath forbidden the adornment of Allah which He hath brought forth for His bondmen, and the good things of His providing" (7,32) "O ye who believe! Forbid not the good things which Allah hath made lawful for you, and transgress not. Lo! Allah loveth not transgressors" (5,87). In the Hadith it is stated "you have a duty toward your Lord, you have a duty toward your body,"[4] in addition to the instructions to maintain cleanliness, small and large ablutions and other rules related to the physical and other conditions.
5. In the field of prevention of diseases, Allah, may He be blessed, says "... and be not cast by your own hands to ruin..." (2,195) "... and eat and drink, but be not prodigal..." (7,31). And He prohibited the harmful foods and beverages such as wine, carcass, blood and pork meat.
   He also prohibited sexual intercourse during menstruation periods and He prohibited the exposure to plagues or whatever causes the spreading of diseases, such as spitting in mosques and public places and relieving oneself at water sources, at the shade and on main roads. He ordered to escape the company of a leper, not to mix sick and healthy camels "not to combine sick ones with those already cured"[5] and not to leave or enter a town inflicted with plague. God instructed to kill dangerous animals and insects and decreed that some of them are impure, aiming that they should be kept away from, and there are many more examples for this in the books.
6. In the field of curing diseases, Allah ordered to get treated, as was related by Aḥmad and the authors of the *Sunan* collections on the authority of the Prophet, who said "Oh God's servants

---

[3] *Ṣaḥīḥ Muslim*, Beirut 1990, v 16, p. 215.
[4] *Ṣaḥīḥ Al-Bukharī*, Cairo 1928, v. 3, p. 87.
[5] Ibn Qayyim, *Zād Al-Maʿād*, v. 3, p. 112.

seek cure, since God did not create a disease for which He created no medicine, except for one—senility." In several traditions, this exceptional disease is either death or boredom. In a relation of Al-Ḥākim "whoever knows what it is—knows, and whoever does not know—does not."[6] In *Ṣaḥīḥ Al-Bukhārī* "God did not reveal a disease had he not revealed its cure" and in *Ṣaḥīḥ Muslim* "each disease has a cure. If the cure for the disease is found, the person recovers with God's permission." And He clarified that seeking the cure does not contradict the trust in God and the acceptance of God's verdicts and submission to Him. In *Sunan Ibn Mājah* it was said to the Messenger of God: do you think that talismans which we resort to and medicines which we use reduce something from God's power?" and he said "they are part of God's power."[7] The Prophet himself used to urge the patients to get cured according to his knowledge, when for example he prescribed honey for someone who suffered belly-aches[8] because God says "wherein is healing for mankind" (16, 69) and he referred the sick to experts in healing such as Al-Ḥārith b. Kalda and his son Al-Naḍr. Many traditions speak of curing some diseases by natural medicines and by spiritual ones which are based on strengthening the soul of the patient and creating trust and hope in getting better. Ibn Qayyim Al-Jawziyya has a whole book about Prophetic medicine, which is part of his greater book *Zād Al-Maʿād fī Hudā Khayr Al-ʿIbād*[9] (the food for the journey to the Hereafter in guidance of the best of all servants) which any scholar of religion and medicine cannot do without.

7. In the realm of treatment, Islam has appointed detailed instructions for the medical staff and for the patient himself and the medicines to cure him. Ibn Qayyim summarized them in 20 points which are the foundation of expertise which must exist in those who work in this profession. Among the most important ones are identifying the type of patient, the reason for that [is to know] how ready the patient is to get cured, according to his natural disposition or his temporary condition, his age and what he/she is used to, while taking into account the seasons and their

---

[6] Ibn Qayyim, *Zād Al-Maʿād*, v. 3, p. 66.
[7] Quoted also in *Zād Al-Maʿād*, v. 3, p. 66, 67.
[8] Ibid., p. 73.
[9] See v. 3 of the Beirut 1982 edition, for example.

worthy *Ṣaḥīḥ*, related by Muslim and others, the Prophet was asked about curing with wine and he said "it is not a medication, it is rather a disease."[15] There are traditions that stress that God would not have decreed the health of the nation of the Prophet to come via things He prohibited. For example, see the tradition of Al-Ṭabarānī and ʿAbd Al-Rāziq "God did not bring about your health via things He forbade upon you."[16] It is also related that a sick person must not be compelled to take a medicine which he/she detests,[17] because mental readiness has much influence on the recovery or on reducing the severity of the disease.

11. After what had been said, let us use the opportunity to comment on what has been published with regard to sex changes via medical treatments and surgeries. The most recent issue is the problem of the medical student at Al-Azhar, named Sayyid ʿAbd Allah, who for a long time has felt feminine inclinations and was treated with many medications, until finally, Dr. ʿIzzat ʿAshm Allah, a specialist at the Umbaba Hospital performed surgery on the student in which his penis was removed, and an opening similar to a vagina was cut in its stead. The student changed his name to Sally, and he became, from his external appearance, a woman. The subject still requires further investigation.

Masculinity has its organs, among the most important of them are the penis, the testicles, the spermatic duct and the prostate which are linked to them. Typical of masculinity at maturity are the attraction to women, the deepening of voice, the appearance of a beard and the small breasts... Femininity has its organs, among the most important ones are the vagina, the womb, the ovaries and the uterine tubes and other parts which are connected to them, and it is typical of women at maturity to be attracted to males, to have treble voices, to grow breasts, not to grow beards, and to menstruate.

Once in a while a person may be born carrying signs of both sexes, then he is defined as an "androgynous" (*khanthā*). If the masculine organs overpower they are exposed via surgery and other techniques and he becomes a male who marries a female and can give birth. If the female organs overpower, they are exposed

---

[15] *Zād Al-Maʿād*, v. 3, p. 114.
[16] Ibid.
[17] *Zād Al-Maʿād*, v. 3, p. 92.

via surgery and other means and she will become a female who will marry a man and may bear children.

However, just having feminine inclinations in a man who is fully equipped with male organs, is a mental condition which does not really turn the man into a woman. These inclinations may be a matter of choice, of desire to look like women, and then they fall into the realm of the prohibited. These may also be uncontrolled inclinations, then they must be treated by all means possible—the treatment might succeed or fail, and it is all depending on God's will. Likewise, masculine inclinations in a woman fully equipped with organs of her sex, are no more than symptoms but do not turn her into a man. Thus she falls into the realm of prohibited acts, if they are a matter of choice, and they must be treated if they are uncontrolled. The trustworthy Hadith dictated to curse the androgynous (*mukhannathīn*) among men and the pretending to be men (*mutarajjilāt*) among women.[18]

12. The operation which was performed on the student Sayyid ʿAbd Allah removed the penis but did not expose feminine organs and the patient thus became neither male nor female. His feminine inclination will never be realized via legitimate sexual intercourse, and Islam does not approve of such a surgery, even if the patient himself gave permission for it. The patient himself has committed a sin.

News has been spread of a man who married and bore children, then became a woman who married and gave birth. If true, then this man was created having both female and male sexual organs. When the male overpowered he married a woman, then they weakened and the others overpowered and he married a man and gave birth. And God is all powerful.

[18] Everett K. Rowson names the *mukhannathūn* "effeminates". For their status in early Islam see his "The Effeminates of Early Medina", in: *Journal of the American Oriental Society*, v. 3, no. 4, October-November 1991, pp. 671-693.

II. Wine Drinking

Maḥmūd Shaltūt, *Al-Fatāwā*
3rd edition, Cairo 1966, pp. 371-373

The reason behind the prohibition of wine

"... When Islam prohibited wine and declared the punishment to those who drink wine, it did not treat wine as a beverage, but rather concentrated on the impact wine has on its drinker such as loss of consciousness which ruins human dignity in man, and which deprives man of the honorable status which Allah granted him. It also ruins relations of love and friendship which should prevail among the individual and other people. It appears permissible when drinking wine to desecrate dignity, to kill people, and it makes turbid the pure knowledge of God's power, which normally grows out of attentiveness and remembrance of His greatness.

These are the main spiritual and social reasons why wine was prohibited. The prohibition is contained and strongly emphasized in the Qur'anic verses 5,90-91 "O ye who believe! Strong drink and games of chance and idols and divining arrows are only an infamy of Satan's handiwork; leave it aside in order that ye may succeed. Satan seeketh only to cast among you enmity and hatred by means of strong drink and games of chance, and to turn you from remembrance of Allah and from (His) worship. Will ye then have done?"

Human research has discovered, in the light of this generous divine revelation, that wine has other dangers aside from these. Doctors have all testified that the liver, the stomach, and other systems suffer from wine, and that alcohol is more responsible for the destruction of humanity than fatal diseases.

Wine is more fatal to man than tuberculosis

I found in my private notes a news item of one of the news agencies of Paris, dated May 1956, which says: The National Institute of Population Census in France, declared today (May 25) that wines started killing more French men and women than tuberculosis. The Institute said: 17,400 Frenchmen died last year from wine, while as only 12,000 died of tuberculosis. Five years ago, the victims of tuberculosis amounted to 26,000, while those of wine 13,000. This is an official report based on statistics of the National French Institute of victims of wine drinking or tuberculosis. This should be a sufficient lesson for those who incline to wine or attempt to deceive people with regard to the position of Islam on wines, and they should understand this so that they comprehend how Allah the all-wise pities them when He prohibits wine and when He describes wine as "an infamy of Satan's handiwork." Is there a greater infamy than that? This all should be added to the economic hazards to the drinker, who transfers the money of the drinker in vain and out of ignorance into the storages of those who manufacture and export wine, and who specialize in advertising it and seducing through it. These damages are in addition to the behavioral hazards of disposal of humility, dignity, respecting the parents, the children and the friends, and in addition to spreading abomination among fathers, sons and grandsons—for which all Islam has prohibited wine.

The prohibition is not limited to the beverage only

These perils of wine, which are obvious and recognized by people, and those that are not obvious, but the expert in the nature of things recognizes, are the reason for the prohibition of wine.

Since the various impacts of wine are reasons for prohibition, the Sharīʿa, which bases its laws on protecting good interests and rejecting damages, must also prohibit any material which might cause similar or worse hazards, whether it is a liquid beverage or a solid food or a smelling powder. This is typical of natural law which man has recognized since he perceived the special qualities of things and compared them with one another, and Islam accepted it too as a system of legislation, and thus it approved the law of the known case to the unknown, because they share common traits.

This renders the laws that appeared concerning any material after the "legislative period" [of the 8-9th centuries] valid, when this material has an impact which is similar or stronger than wine. It is clear that the Prophet's saying "all intoxicating materials are forbidden"[19] is not only a matter of naming, because the Messenger is not a person of words and names, but rather what is meant is that every intoxicating

[19] Dr. Wahba Al-Zuhayly, *Al-Fiqh Al-Islamī wa'Adillatuh*, v. 6, p. 149.

material falls under the law of wine as far as prohibition and punishment are concerned.

Consequently, from what has been observed and is now known, "drugs" such as hashish, opium and cocaine, which contain dangers to the health, brain, spirit, conduct, economics and society even more so than wine, in the view of Islam, must also be prohibited. If it is not stated by a literal text then it is according to the spirit and general meaning and according to the general axiom which is the first foundation of legislation in Islam: prevention of damage and blocking the means of corruption.

III. Drugs and Pork-Meat

Risālat Al-Islām, March 1986, pp. 49-50
"Why did Islam prohibit the use of drugs and pork-meat?"

The prohibition of using drugs

God may He be exalted says:

> Spend your wealth for the cause of Allah, and be not cast by your own hands to ruin; and do good. Lo! Allah loveth the beneficent. (Qur'an 2,195)

Ruin is what leads to destruction. Drugs, no doubt lead to destruction, and therefore they are totally forbidden in all their types, whether it is hashish, opium, morphine shots, heroin, hallucinogenics, or anything which has a destructive impact on the soundness of the mind and the sensitivity toward humane values and an assessment of the commitment to obey Allah and the Messenger which are the greatest graces bestowed by Allah on man.

Addiction to drugs creates for the addict a world far away from real life. All the sensations there are false. Feelings of happiness or joy are in reality a fall into the worst conditions of abandonment of human nature and of self humiliation which people can find themselves in. The influence of drugs is not only limited to damaging the brain and the unconsciousness, but it reaches the body too and influences the heart muscle and heartbeat regularity. Exaggeration might lead to a stroke. Likewise, an addict who takes drugs intraveneously can be inflicted with pathogenic blood poisoning (sepsis), and contagious liver inflammation (hepatitis).

As a result of drug addiction the health deteriorates and the body's immunization system loses its ability to function, because of the recurring instances of unconsciousness, the loss of appetite and the deprivation of the body from regular meals.

Thus, drug addiction results in thinness, loss of strength and these are followed by worsening of behavior and thinking, exposure to attacks of fury and loss of control, especially in those who take hallucinatory pills.

Under the influence of these pills unusually brutal crimes have been committed, and there is no doubt that the most dangerous thing today for Western society is the spread of these pills and the drugs marijuana and heroin.

Addiction reached unbelievable dimensions and entailed a dangerous increase in crime and violence. The preachers against the collapse of society in these countries have started to speak of it, since the rulers have felt a loss of control and of values. Bestial instincts in behavior and thought have started to take over. The family ties disintegrated and the religious inhibition as well as the behavioral and moral restrictions disappeared. In time this will cause the ruin of these countries and the vanishing of their civilizations.

The prohibition of eating pork-meat

Allah prohibited for the believers the eating of pork-meat, by his saying: "O ye who believe! Eat of the good things wherewith we have provided you and render thanks to Allah if it is (indeed) He whom ye worship" (Qur'an 2,172).

The prohibition of eating pork-meat is intended by Allah to protect His servants from harm that could befall them, had they eaten the meat of this impure animal. The study of parasitology explains that there is one type of worm called Taenia and there are two types of it the Taenia saginata (tape cattle worm) and the tape swine's worm (Taenia solium), and there are many similarities between the two types with respect to form and to life-cycle and to the way a person is afflicted with this contagious disease. This is so because the Taenia worm, whether it is tape cattle worm or tape swine worm, lives in the small intestine of humans. The existence of tape swine worm in the human intestine can create a very dangerous disease called cysticercosis. This disease does not attack whoever abstains from eating pork-meat. While as the tape cattle worm does not bring about such severe complications.

The severity of this disease is that it creates damage to the heart muscle or the eye or the brain or the muscles, and the symptoms that might appear are a decrease of heart beat and failure of the blood circulation or loss of vision or paralysis or epilepsy.

Another disease that may attack the human being because of eating pork-meat is called trichinosis, the symptoms of which are vomiting, diarrhea, abdominal colic pains. Generally in the body it might cause edema in the eyes, pain in the muscles, high fever, swelling of the skin, difficulty in breathing, and in the most extreme cases, it can cause death because of lung inflammation and a sharp decrease of heart beat.

The Muslim, when he obeys Allah, may He be praised and exalted, and does not eat pork-meat, respects his/her human dignity and takes pride in the purity of his/her body, and does not eat the meat of an impure animal which lives on rubbish and garbage and does not abstain from eating the meat of dead mice or dead swine. Allah ordered the believers to eat good foods, and prohibited defilement in His saying in Qur'an 2,172 (as quoted above).

IV. Smoking

Fatāwā ʿAbd Al-Ḥalīm Maḥmūd
2nd edition, Cairo n.d., v. 2, p. 266
"Islam's attitude to smoking"

Some people's health and body can tolerate smoking, and cigarettes do not cause them damage, no matter how many they smoke. Smoking does not cause harm from the aspect of their own sustenance and their family's sustenance. In such a case smoking is reprehensible (*makrūh*), because it entails spending money on a useless item. Spending money in vain is not a sign of well balanced, calm and reasonable people. Therefore, smoking in such a case is rated only as reprehensible, i.e. it is not prohibited.

However, if the situation is different and smoking becomes harmful to the health, it is prohibited and smoking is then a sin, and an offence if smoking disturbs the dependents of the smoker. This is similar to as if he was in poverty and needed money to spend on his family for housing, clothing and food, or for treating a sick person in the family—in such a case smoking is also prohibited. It is a sin for a man to neglect his dependents by spending money on useless items.

Every leader is responsible for his subjects. Responsibility, as much as it is a must from the literary and reformatory aspects, it is also a must on the materialistic aspect of sustaining, healing and providing housing and food. Smoking is a type of spending. God may He be praised and exalted says in the Qur'an: "... but be not prodigal. Lo! He loveth not the prodigals" (7,31) and He also says: "Lo! the squanderers were ever brothers of the devils..." (17,27).

We conclude from all this that the verdict toward smoking depends on the individual's condition. The general rule is what the Messenger of Allah said: "no harm and no damage", i.e., the human being must keep away from anything that can harm himself or can bring about harm to others.

Maḥmūd Shaltūt, *Al-Fatāwā*
3rd edition, Cairo 1966, pp. 383-385
"Smoking"

Views of scholars about tobacco

Tobacco was not known in Muslim countries until the beginning of the 11th century Hijrī, that is roughly for 400 years. Therefore none of the medieval jurists spoke of it, not to mention those who preceded them. Consequently, it was neither prohibited nor permitted.

The scholars at the time tobacco appeared spoke of it, but did not come to an agreement vis-a-vis its legitimacy, similarly to their habit with every new matter which was not known at the time of legal codification. Some of them decreed it was permitted, because it was not intoxicating, and could not intoxicate, and considering that it is not harmful to everybody who tries it. The basic rule in such matters is permission, and it is only prohibited to those who are harmed and influenced by it.

Those who prohibit or say it is reprehensible have a strong claim

Other scholars decreed it is prohibited or reprehensible, relying on what is known about it, that is, it weakens the health of the smoker and makes him/her lose their appetite, and exposes his/her vital faculties or most of them to disorder and trouble, especially the heart and the lungs. One of the principles of Islam is that prohibitions are intended either to defend the creed, or the mind or the property or the dignity. Prohibition or reprehension are relative to the weakening of any of these aspects. Whenever the danger is greater, the prohibition is stronger, and whatever is less harmful is less prohibited. Physical health is not less important than mental health or property, with regard to caring for it. Often Islam prohibits things when it foresees that their damage in the future might increase. Moreover, it even prohibits the fulfillment of commandments when it is certain that it causes harm or doubles the harm.

The risks of smoking to health and property require that it be prevented

While tobacco is not intoxicating and does not cause damage to the mind, it nevertheless has harmful effects to the health of both the smoker and non-smoker. Doctors analyzed its elements and identified the toxic element, which ruins—though very slowly—the happiness and pleasure of man. Thus there is no doubt of the damage and risk. Causing damage is in the view of Islam an abomination that needs to be avoided. If we add to that the amounts of money spent on it, which very often the smoker could use otherwise, that is in more useful and productive directions. From this respect, smoking has an economic side which in the eyes of the Sharīʿa requires that it be prevented and not permitted.

Based on our strong recognition of the negative impacts of tobacco on both health and property, we learn that Islamic law despises it and finds it reprehensible. The decision of Islam that something is prohibited or reprehensible does not depend on the existence of a specific text speaking of it. The legal rationale and the general principles of legislation have their value in understanding the law. These reasons and principles prepared Islam well to match anything new which people invent. The verdict as to whether it is permitted or prohibited is made via identifying specifications and common traits, and wherever there is damage, there should also be prevention. Whenever benefit can be drawn or is predominant, there should also be permission. Whenever the benefit and damage are equal prevention is preferred to treatment.[20]

---

[20] As a matter of fact, when an act results in an equal benefit (*nafʿ*) or damage (*ḍarar*), scholars are divided as to what should be done. Dr. Ḥusayn Ḥāmid Ḥussān,

The duty of governments

Since it is the duty of enlightened governments which care for their subjects to block the means of damage in a general manner, it is obligatory and necessary for those governments to defend youngsters from whatever damages their health. There is no doubt that the youngsters' systems are more easily influenced than others and cannot combat this slow poison. This is the law concerning the smoking of tobacco, and similarly the law concerning planting and manufacturing it, as long as no other uses than smoking of tobacco are known.

V. Banks of Milk

Al-Jumʿa, March-April 1988, pp. 25-26

Islamic law and banks for the sale of mothers' milk

> The spread of these banks leads to the spread of diseases and to the disruption of the genealogical lines.

The subject of "mothers' milk banks" has been discussed recently, as well as the position of Islamic law toward these banks which collect or buy mothers' milk, then mix it and sell it for the nourishment of babies, instead of breast-feeding or feeding by wet-nurses.

Several important questions are related to the establishment of these banks and their legitimacy. The first question is whether Islamic law permits a child to feed from such milk? Is it permitted to sell mother's milk, or not? What is the law concerning the prohibition to marry among those who were breast-fed by the same woman? What results may follow the feeding of a child with milk collected from several mothers?

All these questions, and more, are discussed in a book which was published recently by *Al-Azhar* magazine, entitled "The position of Islamic law toward banks for the sale of mothers' milk." The author of the book is Dr. Ramaḍān Ḥāfiẓ ʿAbd Al-Raḥmān Al-Asyūṭī, a Professor of Law at the Islamic and General Law Department in Al-Azhar.

Uṣūl Al-Fiqh, Cairo 1970, p. 359. Shaltūt, it appears, chose the safest way to prevent damage—prohibition.

The author says in the introduction to the book that what made him discuss the subject is its importance, its severe danger, its great criminality and the great harm it can inflict upon the Islamic nation. "Banks for the sale of mother's milk" is a new phenomenon, around which many questions and inquiries have arisen. The answers to them are contradictory.

The author starts with the definition of "breast-feeding" from a legal as well as from a lexical aspect. Lexically "breast-feeding" is a noun which means the sucking of the breast and drinking its milk. Legally it means that human milk reaches a wide place which is believed to be the place of other foods.

The author proves the prohibition to marry among those breast-fed together by claiming that the Qur'an and the Sunna both prohibited such marriages as appears in the verse

> and your mothers who breast-fed you, and your sisters who were breast-fed with you. (4,23)

The author of *Al-Mughnī*[21] also said

> the scholars unanimously agreed upon the prohibition [of marriage] by breast-feeding.

The reason for the prohibition of marriage because of being breast-fed together is that breast-feeding is based on the principle that

> whoever breast-feeds is likened with a mother since she is responsible for the gathering of tissues, i.e. the combination of the body build-up and skeleton; while as the mother is responsible for the body build-up in her womb, the wet-nurse supplies the baby's nourishment during the first stage of its growth; she is therefore a mother after the [biological] mother and her children are brothers after the [biological] brothers.

Breast-feeding is concerned with four elements: the individual suction, the suckling baby, the milk and the form of breast-feeding. The author meticulously explains the conditions which correspond to each of the four principles.

With regard to breast-feeding with mixed milk, the author finds two problems:

a. If the wet-nurse's milk is mixed with something of a different sort such as an animal's milk, or honey or melted butter or food or liquid—if the wet-nurse's milk equals the added material or is

[21] Abū Muḥammad ʿAbd Allah b. Aḥmad b. Muḥammad b. Qudāma (d. 1223).

more than it quantitatively, the prohibition [to marriage] prevails. However, if the added milk is more than the original milk—the prohibition does not prevail.

b. If the wet-nurse's milk is mixed with another milk, such as another woman's milk—the prohibition [to marriage] prevails, regardless of whether the other woman's milk equals, that is whether it is more or less, is irrelevant.

The author says that selling mother's milk or giving it as a gift are among the dangerous transactions which are surrounded with harm and shortcomings. What harm and what trial are more severe than a sale which leads to the disruption of genealogy and to the desecration of honor, which all legal systems agreed upon the necessity to preserve?

The author said that banks for the sale of mother's milk are the *bid'a* (undesired innovation) of our times.[22] The author resorted to sayings of scholars of the four schools of law (the Ḥanafī, Shāfiʿī, Mālikī and Ḥanbalī) to prove his stand. After clarifying the views of the scholars, the author emphasized that "all of them, i.e. all four types of scholars, are unanimously against any sale which entails harm or leads to corruption or sin and consequently it is forbidden by Islamic law. Therefore, mixture of mothers' milk leads to a wrong act, moreover, to a very wrong act, because it leads to the mingling of the genealogical lines which Allah ordered to protect.

Dr. Ramaḍān Al-Asyūṭī concludes by saying

> that he prohibits the sale of mother's milk as well as its remuneration. He also prohibits donating the milk because all this leads to the mingling of genealogical lines.

He relies on a legal principle according to which when the necessity (*ḍarūra*) conflicts with an obstacle the obstacle should be given priority.[23]

The necessity is of the breast-feeding, the obstacle is the mingling of genealogical lines and the violation of marriages.

As for the donation of milk, the author says that donations are permitted legally, moreover they are recommended. But if the donation

---

[22] See Vardit Rispler, "Toward a New Understanding of the Term *bid'a*", in: *Der Islam*, v. 2, 1991, pp. 320-328.

[23] For the status of *ḍarūrāt* in Islamic law, see: Muḥammad Abū Zuhra, *Uṣūl Al-Fiqh*, Cairo 1957, pp. 370-373.

leads to a foul act, then it is prohibited by Islamic law. Whatever leads to a prohibited act is prohibited too. Therefore, it is not acceptable to donate mother's milk to banks for mother's milk, since this leads to mingling genealogical lines. Consequently, any milk donation leads to mingling genealogical lines, to invalidation of marriage and to the spread of adultery, and therefore it is forbidden. The author added that sale of milk or its donation is a plot of the Jews which is intended to ruin the genealogy of Muslims and exterminate them.

The author also responds to those who permitted the establishment of banks for sale of mothers' milk, saying that they claimed *riḍāʿ* means sucking and drinking the breast's milk and that drinking milk not from the breast is not considered *riḍāʿ*. Dr. Al-Asyūṭī says that drinking milk, whether from the breast or from a vessel is legally the same act. Islamic law is bound by legal definitions, not by lexical ones. The prohibition for marriage is linked to the material—milk, not to its source which is the breast. This is supported by a hadith transmitted by Abū Dā'ūd on the authority of the son of Abū Masʿūd that the Prophet said

> "*riḍāʿ* is the act which stretches the bones and makes the flesh grow",[24] these two attributes are characteristics of the milk, and are not related to the breast.

Dr. Al-Asyūṭī explained the implications of banks of mother's milk and said that they lead to the commitment of crimes, deterioration of moral conduct, confusion of genealogical lines and the spread of adultery, plagues and harm to human dignity.

The problem of banks of mother's milk remains pending among the jurists ... at a time when the gates of *ijtihād* (independent reasoning) are still closed ... what is the position of Dr. Muḥammad Sayyid Ṭanṭāwī, the *muftī* of the Republic, and what is the position of Dr. ʿAbd Allah Al-Mushidd, the Chairman of the Fatwā Committee, and what is the position of the physicians' spokesman on the spread of such banks?

---

[24] Dr. Wahba Al-Zuhayly, *Al-Fiqh Al-Islami wa'Adillatuh*, v. 7, p. 141.

Hudā Al-Islām, No. 5, February-March 1992, p. 95
Sheikh Yūsuf ʿAbd Al-Wahhāb Abū Snīna,
Imām Al-Masjid Al-Aqṣā, Jerusalem

Question: Should a woman be compelled to breast-feed her child?

Answer: Several scholars claim that the mother must breast-feed her child, as required by Qurʾan 2,233: "Mothers shall suckle their children." It is also an order according to the grammatic form in which it was stated [in the Qurʾan].

It is the position of the Mālikī school that the mother must breast-feed if she is married, or if the child refuses to suckle from another woman's breast, or if there is no father. Excluded from these cases is the woman who according to local custom is believed to be a descendent of the Prophet (*sharīfa*). In the case of a divorcee whose divorce is irrevocable—the husband is responsible for the nursing, unless the mother wishes to breast-feed the child, for which act she is entitled to a payment equal to that of a wet-nurse.[25]

Most jurists leave the subject in the level of recommendation (*nadb*) [not a must], and say that the mother must breast-feed her child only if the child cannot accept another woman's milk or when the father is unable to hire a wet-nurse for the child, or when the father is capable [financially] but cannot find a wet-nurse. This is based on Qurʾan 65,6

> ... but if ye make difficulties for one another, then let some other woman give suck for him (the father of the child).[26]

If breast-feeding were obligatory Islamic law would have forced her to do it, but it only recommended the mother should breast-feed, because the mother's milk is better for the child and his mother's compassion upon him/her is thus greater. And Allah knows best.

---

[25] Dr. Wahba Al-Zuhayly, *Al-Fiqh Al-Islami wa'Adillatuh*, v. 7, pp. 700-704.
[26] Ibid., v. 7, p. 699.

VI. Sex During Menstruation

Ḥasanayn Muḥammad Makhlūf
Fatāwā Sharʿiyya wa Buḥūth Islāmiyya
3rd edition, Cairo 1971, v. 1, pp. 225-227

The wisdom in the instruction to keep away from the menstruating woman (ḥāʾiḍ)

Question: The verse 2,222 reads:

> They question thee (o Muhammad) concerning menstruation. Say: It is an illness, so let women alone at such times and go not in unto them till they are cleansed. And when they have purified themselves, then go in unto them as Allah hath enjoined upon you. Truly Allah loveth those who turn unto Him, and loveth those who have a care for cleanness.

What is the wisdom in keeping away from women, and is it mandatory to behave thus?

Answer: It is related on the authority of Anas b. Mālik, may Allah be pleased with him, that the Jews used to send the menstruating woman out of the house, and would not eat or drink with her. They would also not associate with her in the house, that is they would not befriend her. The Messenger of God was asked about it, and God revealed this verse in response, and then said the Prophet:

> You may associate with them inside the house and do everything but not sexual relations.

And God's word (keep away!) in the imperative means that it is mandatory, and entails keeping away from normal sex with women during their period, and the prohibition of penetration. Allah emphasized this in His words

> and go not in unto them till they are cleansed. And when they have purified themselves, then go in unto them (etc.)

The Qurʿan declared the reason for this law by His saying "it is an illness", i.e. contaminated or harmful, and therefore abhorrent to human nature.

It is mentioned in the Hadith that sexual intercourse during menses, i.e. persistence on it, brings about leprosy to the fetus and therefore it is harmful.[27]

The doctors say

> during menses the cervix opens so that blood can come out, and the acidity of the vagina decreases and the immunization of the reproductive system against pathogens is weakened. Therefore there cannot be done any vaginal examination or an insertion of a finger or intercourse during menses, because this could lead to the insertion of pathogens into the womb and through it to the peritoneum which can cause severe inflammations with serious results.

They say that menses blood in cases of chronic inflammations contains pathogens secreted by uterus glands. These pathogens are being developed during the month, and at the time of menses they grow and multiply and mix with menses blood, and intercourse at this period causes the man to be inflicted with sexual inflammations.

Aḥmad [b. Ḥanbal], Al-Tirmidhī and Al-Nisāʾī relate on the authority of Abū Hurayra who quotes the Prophet who said

> whoever has sexual intercourse with a menstruating woman is considered one who denied (*kafara*) what was revealed to Muhammad.[28]

The usage of the term *kufr* is understood as saying that having sexual intercourse with this woman is forbidden, or that it is intended to exaggerate the reproach and warning. This is not contradicted by another tradition related by Al-Ṭabarānī on the authority of Ibn ʿAbbās, may Allah be pleased with both, who said: "a man came to the Prophet and told him: I had intercourse with my wife during her menses, and the Messenger of God ordered him to release one slave"[29] [as compensation]. Al-Shāfiʿī determines that such is a major sin, and God knows best.[30]

---

[27] A summary of the medical hazards that await the man and woman that have sexual intercourse during menses can be found in Dr. Muḥammad Bakr Ismāʿīl, *Al-Fiqh Al-Wāḍiḥ*, Cairo 1990, v. 1, pp. 105-108. No hazards to the fetus are mentioned in it.

[28] *Sunan Ibn Mājah*, 3rd edition, Riyad 1988, v. 1, p. 105.

[29] Muḥammad Al-Muntaṣir Al-Kattānī, *Muʿjam Fiqh Al-Salaf*, Mecca 1984, v. 1, p. 132. The release of a slave is the least mentioned option of compensation. Monetary compensation is more common.

[30] The jurists are divided as to how severe the punishment should be. Most of them think that (*istighfār*) asking forgiveness and expressing regret is a sufficient com-

VII. Freezing Sperm

Al-Iʿtiṣām, June 1989, no. 3
Dhū Al-Qaʿda 1409, pp. 38-39

The position of religion about a woman who preserves her husband's sperm... Is it permitted to artificially fertilize the wife's ovum with her husband's sperm? by A.D. Muḥammad Muṣṭafā Shalabī.[31]

In the newspaper *Al-Nūr*, no. 350 of 6 Rabīʿ Al-Ākhir 1409/ November 16, 1988, under column "laws and fatāwā" which were answered by the dignified Sheikh ʿAbd Allah Al-Mushidd, the head of the Fatwā Committee at Al-Azhar ... and when I read those answers I was astonished at their content ... and I wish to express my viewpoint in order to do justice to the Lord who is greater than me or him.

The first question says: "What is the position of religion about a woman who preserves her husband's sperm to be used after his death, in order to bear children?"

The answer of the honorable Sheikh [Al-Mushidd] was: If it is verified with no doubt that pregnancy was generated by her husband's sperm, there is nothing wrong. However, if there is any doubt that the sperm was replaced by another's, then it is forbidden to use it, in order to protect the genealogical lines.

God for the same reason prohibited adultery, in order to avoid confusion of genealogical lines.

The Sheikh only stipulated in his answer that the sperm is verified beyond doubt to be the husband's ... Deriving from this, that nothing is wrong if the wife does this for several years, even in her last years of reproduction.

This is anarchy which no mind or religion can approve ... regardless of whether this can happen or the reasons which may bring it about. The Sheikh, unlike his other answers, did not mention any sources or proof ... Sharʿī laws, in order to be valid, must rely on a true reference. The Sheikh had already answered the same answer to a question

---

pensation. Others and Al-Shāfiʿī among them require a monetary fine of one half or one dinar, depending on the stage of menstruation. See: *Sunan Abī Dā'ūd*, 1st edition, Beirut 1969, v. 1, p. 181.

[31] A member of the Islamic Research Council, Professor emeritus of law in Cairo Faculty of Sharīʿa. Professor and Chairman of Islamic Law departments at both the Universities of Alexandria and Beirut.

addressed to him a little differently: "is it permissible to artificially fertilize a woman's ovum with her husband's sperm during the *ʿidda* (waiting period) after his death?," and he said it was permissible according to the Sharīʿa...

When the Islamic Research Council expressed reservations to that *fatwā* and showed it was mistaken, the Sheikh responded to the reservation in a note in which he justified his *fatwā* according to his point of view, and said: This fertilization is permitted by the Sharīʿa, based on the general rule that originally things are permitted if most scholars agree, i.e. Al-Shāfiʿī, Mālik, Aḥmad. The author of *Al-Hidāya*,[32] the Ḥanafī, rejected the procedure because he could not find a Sharʿī support which permitted or prohibited it, therefore, it is neutral ... not prohibited by itself.

[The reasons for permission are] because there is no decisive text, and it is also not prohibited because of another thing, since this is not a means which leads to a prohibited act, and because it nevertheless preserves the remnants of the previous marriage after the husband's death, such as his bequest, and the *ʿidda* and the stability of genealogical lines for one year after the date of death.

The Sheikh also resorted to a *fatwā* issued by Dār Al-Iftāʾ at the time of Jād Al-Ḥaqq which permitted to fertilize the ovum of the wife with her husband's sperm during his lifetime, if it is verified as his.

I was asked during the debate between the Islamic Research Council and Sheikh Al-Mushidd to write a memorandum and clarify the truth in this and other controversial problems among us, and I wrote regarding all disputed issues and I still keep it and never offered it to the Council because for other reasons the Council has been closed now for more than two years. I will therefore summarize now from the memorandum my answer:

I told the Sheikh: if we agree with you that the principle of all things among the jurists is to permit—as said before—we will ask you a specific question: Does the status of the divorcee not remain as it is after the husband's death, so that she can legally obtain such a fertilization which leads to the birth of a child? You will not be able to claim that permission is granted because the status of "divorcee" was terminated by death?!

Your claim that some impacts of the previous marriage, such as bequest, *ʿidda*, and the continuation of genealogical affiliation are still

---

[32] Abū Al-Ḥasan ʿAlī b. Abī Bakr b. ʿAbd Al-Jalīl Al-Rushdānī Al-Marghīnānī (d. 1197).

existent if the child is born within a year from the date of the husband's death—a period sufficient to indicate whether the child was in existence then, or not—this claim does not justify your *fatwā*. Because these impacts are laws which the Legislator laid in many verses assuming this marriage took place during the lifetime of the husband. There is no verse or proof for the legitimacy of insemination. As for your insistence that the general rule is permission ... it does not serve your cause ... because the problem is not only fertilizing the ovum with the dead husband's sperm and that is all... the act entails also pregnancy and birth ... and your *fatwā* approving that such insemination is legitimate during the wife's *ʿidda*, necessarily implies that the insemination may be conducted even at the last moment of the *ʿidda* ... and if the woman is then impregnated and gives birth after her *ʿidda* has ended, which is after a year of 365 days ... do you still claim that the genealogy of the child ties him/her to his/her dead father, thus you extend the genealogical order with the support of a Sharʿī reason! This is a forbidden issue, not agreed upon by any jurist. In addition to that, this contradicts your previous claim and the fact that the genealogical ties remain steady in a period during which it can be known that the child was existent at the father's death, which is one year as is common today.

If you deny the genealogical ties of the child, then your *fatwā* sends out to the world forlorn children, whose status is worse than that of foundlings. Because the foundling may still find a person who would claim to be his father and identify his/her genealogy with that of whoever claimed to be the father, if certain conditions that the jurists enumerated for claiming blood ties are fulfilled ... As for this child—no-one can claim him/her for himself/herself, unless the deceased came out of the grave and claimed to be his/her father.

Your finding support in a *fatwā* which permitted the insemination of the wife's ovum with the husband's sperm during his lifetime, if the sperm is verified as his—does not help you ... because it is an incomplete analogy ... (*qiyās*). There has to be a husband, a wife and a marital bed (*firāsh*) ... this is a term stipulated by the jurists unanimously for the genealogical ties to remain steady. The Messenger of God said "the child belongs to the bed [of a married couple] and the stone [stoning] belongs to the prostitute." This is not mentioned in the question part of the *fatwā*.

Even if we ignore all that has been said and assume such an act is permissible based on that "the principle of all things is permission"—

permission may prohibit things that result in great damage based on [another] a known legal principle of "blocking the means" (*sadd al-dharā'i'*)[33] [for a negative act]. Broadcasting this *fatwā* among people may lead widowed women to walk a thorny road. Once a widow becomes pregnant, she will claim it is from the heritage of her late husband who left her his sperm to be used after his death for insemination—all based on this *fatwā*, oh Sheikh 'Abd Allah Al-Mushidd!

This is enough damage to stop this permission and withdraw from this *fatwā*. If we have justified hereby the invalidity of your first *fatwā* which permitted insemination during *'idda*, this *fatwā* which permits insemination after death, is shown to be much more invalid. And God knows best.

VIII. About Masturbation

Fatāwā 'Abd Al-Ḥalīm Maḥmūd
2nd edition, Cairo n.d., v. 2, p. 244

Masturbation is a disease quite common among boys. It is an ancient disease, known among some irresponsible Arabs and among others.

When Mālik [b. Anas] was asked about it he recited God's words "And who guard their modesty—save from their wives or the slaves that their right hands possess, for then they are not blameworthy" (23, 5-6). God limited the means to releasing semen to the Shar'ī marriage or to the female slaves one owns. Anything beyond this permission is forbidden and improper. However, masturbation is permitted when the need for that is very strong, because it is considered the release of waste matter from the body which is like blood letting.

But most scholars determined that it is prohibited, several even claimed that the masturbator is like someone committing adultery with oneself.[34] Al-Qurṭubī said: it is a crime invented by Satan and

---

[33] See an elaborate discussion of *dharā'i'* (means) in Islamic law in Muḥammad Abū Zuhra, *Uṣūl Al-Fiqh*, Cairo 1957, pp. 287-295.

[34] Masturbation according to another definition is one's marrying his hand... It is a crime which requires punishment, but not as severe as *ḥadd*, rather a *ta'zīr*. Masturbation is less severe than adultery because it does not entail mixture of genealogical lines and public corruption. See: 'Abd al-Raḥmān Al-Jazīrī, *Al-Fiqh 'alā Al-Madhāhib Al-Arba'a*, Cairo 1990, v. 5, p. 123.

spread among people, until it became an accepted thing.[35] If only it were not so...

If proof were provided that it is a permissible act, men should have turned away from it because of its baseness. Many doctors warned against the dangers which masturbation poses to the body: to the sexual drive, to the faculty of sight and the respiratory system, etc., and they prescribed the ways to escape the risks of masturbation, as practicing sports, meeting people and participation in various activities which make one stop thinking of masturbation.

We can add to that the encouragement to fast and fulfill religious duties, approaching religious scholars in order to oppress desire and remove thoughts on this subject.

The most effective treatment which pleases Allah and His Messenger is definitely marriage. If a person turns to Allah begging sincerely that Allah will make sustenance and marriage easier for him, and if he tries hard to make money in proper ways, then Allah may He be praised will open the ways for him and will facilitate his livelihood.

Muḥammad Mutawallī Al-Shaʿrāwī
Al-Fatāwā kull mā Yahimm Al-Muslim fī Ḥayātihi waYawmihi waGhaddihi
1-10, Cairo n.d., pp. 326-327

A medical problem

Question: Is it permitted or prohibited to masturbate? Does it cause tuberculosis to the boy or girl who practises it, as some people say, and does excessive masturbation have harmful side-effects on the rest of the body organs?

Answer: Masturbation is an improper behavior which young boys and girls close to sexual maturity resort to during the dream periods which are often influenced by the sexual hormones, the secretion of which in the body is stimulated by the seminal glands.

---

35 In Al-Qurṭubī, *Al-Jāmiʿ liAḥkām Al-Qurʿān*, Cairo 1967, v. 12, pp. 105-106, according to Aḥmad b. Ḥanbal only, masturbation is permissible as it is a release of bodily material which is superfluous. "Several scholars claim it is like having sexual intercourse with oneself which is a sin created by Satan and spread among people in such a manner that it becomes normative..."

The increase in sexual desire is probably a result of the increase of the hormonal level on the one hand, and on the other hand because the conservative religious society does not allow an un Sharʿī release of these charges and powerful energies. Both lead to depression which is quite common, and the teenagers may suffer from neurosis, i.e. strong emotional tension which overpowers all their conduct and movements vis-à-vis the development of their life.

To do justice to science we say that masturbation has no impact on the organs, but it is a bad indecent habit, and people most likely do it because of their having too much freetime, they are irresponsible and indifferent.

It is not true, rather it is an exaggeration, that whoever masturbates becomes sick with tuberculosis or blindness.

In order to get rid of this indecent, despicable habit one has to occupy oneself with continuous, permanent work, by fasting and by reading the Qur'an until circumstances allow one to marry, which is the natural cure for this problem.

IX. Epilepsy of the Wife and its Implications

Al-Fatāwā Al-Islāmiyya
Dar Al-Iftā' Al-Miṣriyya
v.8, 1983, pp. 2993-2995
The *muftī* is Jād Al-Ḥaqq ʿAlī Jād Al-Ḥaqq
and the date of publication is May 13, 1980

Principles

1. A request to annul the marital contract when one of the spouses is found to be an invalid is not permissible by the Ẓāhirīs,[36] regardless whether the handicap was found before or after the contract was issued.
2. The appearance of specific health defects in the man allow the wife to request separation, according to Ḥanafī jurists. Mālikī Shāfiʿī and Ḥanbalī jurists think that the husband and wife have equal rights to request separation.[37]

---

[36] A school of law named after Dā'ud Khalaf Al-Ẓāhirī (d. 882), who based his formulations on literal interpretations of texts only.

[37] Legally, husband and wife have equal rights to request separation. See: *Al-Fiqh*

3. If a defect was found in the wife after consummation, of which the husband was not aware of before the marriage contract was prepared, and of which he was not pleased, the husband may request the dower from the person who deceived him; this is the accepted view according to the Ḥanbalīs, and this was also the stand of Mālikīs and Shāfiʿīs in early times.[38] A new verdict of Shāfiʿīs and Ḥanafīs concludes that nothing can be withdrawn after consummation.[39]
4. The most prominent view according to the Ḥanafīs is that a man may not request the annulment of marriage if he found a defect in his wife, and he cannot request any of the dower from anybody. The state law acts according to these guidelines.

Question: Request No. 360 year 1979 says that the son of the asker married a woman, and after consummation he was surprised to find out that she was epileptic. The epileptic seizures recurred and the mentioned husband understood that his wife's parents concealed the fact which they had known before he married their daughter until the marriage was conducted and consummation followed.

After becoming pregnant by her husband, she had a miscarriage and the physicians concluded that the reason for the miscarriage was her infliction with this disease and that she might always suffer from it, and that even if she became pregnant in the future she would give birth to a deformed fetus. The asker requested the clarification of the sharʿī viewpoint about this marriage and of her father's liability from a civil and Sharʿī points of view, since he had concealed this fact. What are the rights of the husband in such a case?

ʿalā Al-Madhāhib Al-Arbaʿa, 1990, v. 4, pp. 265-266. Practically divorce is in the hands of the husband because "as smart as the woman may be, she is apt to be emotionally moved and does not have patience like man and might use separation too often thus ruin the couple's life." Ibid. p. 332.

[38] The wife must return the dower herself, if her physical defect was concealed by her from her guardian. If, however, the defect was visible so that the guardian could know about it, the guardian has to return the dower, not the wife. See: Dr. Wahba Al-Zuhayly, *Al-Fiqh Al-Islamī wa'Adillatuh*, 3rd edition, Damascus 1989, v. 7, pp. 523-525.

[39] The terminology *ṣaḥīḥ jadīd* (sound and new) appears also for example in Ibn Kathīr, *Tafsīr Ibn Kathīr*, Cairo 1924, v. 1, p. 512. I am grateful to Prof. H. Lazarus-Yaffe for this reference.

Answer: Marriage in Islam is based on love, compassion and mutual dignified companionship. If one of the two spouses suddenly develops health defects which are permanent and incurable —is it permitted by law to one of them to request annulment of marriage, or not?

The Sharīʿā jurists are divided into three groups:

1. There is no option to any of the spouses when he/she discovered a health defect in the other. He may not request annulment of marriage regardless if the defect existed before the contract or happened after it was signed, and regardless if the defect is in the husband or the wife. This is the position of the Ẓāhiriyya.
2. Separation may be requested with the existence of certain defects. This is the viewpoint of Ḥanafī, Mālikī, Shāfiʿī and Ḥanbalī jurists. The Ḥanafī jurists, however, think that separation can occur because of health defects found specifically in the man; they differ as to how many defects there should be. The jurists of the Mālikī, Shāfiʿī, Ḥanbalī, Zaydī and Jaʿfarī schools of law permit the request of separation because of health defects found in both men and women, but they too differ with regard to the number of defects which justify the request and their kind.
3. The request of separation is permitted to all because of any health or physical defect, and both spouses have this right. This is the position of Shurayḥ, Ibn Shihāb, Al-Zuhrī and Abū Thawr. Ibn Qayyim supported this viewpoint in *Zād Al-Maʿād*, v. 4, pp. 58, 59.

According to the Ḥanbalī school, the common view, as expressed by Ibn Qudāma in *Al-Mughnī*, v. 7, p. 587, if the husband found a defect in his wife after consummation, a defect which he had not been aware of before the contract of marriage and which he was unhappy about— he could request the dower from whoever deceived him, since the guardian of the wife is liable for the dower. This is the position of Mālik, Shāfiʿī in old times, Al-Zuhrī and Qatāda, with reference to a tradition attributed to ʿUmar b. Al-Khaṭṭāb. Abū Ḥanīfa and Shafiʿī in recent generations said that the husband may not request anything from anybody, because by consummation of marriage his right was already fulfilled, based on a saying of ʿAlī b. Abī Ṭālib on such a case.[40]

[40] The same idea is related by Ibn ʿUmar and Saʿīd b. Jubayr. See: *Ṣaḥīḥ Al-Bukhārī*, 4th edition, Beirut 1985, v. 7, pp. 198-200.

Jurisdiction in Egypt followed in this case the most prevalent opinions of the Ḥanafī school, acting according to article 280 of the regulations of the Sharʿī courts, decree-law no. 78 year 1931.

According to the legal perception of this school of law the husband has no right to compensation when requesting the annulment of marriage if he found any defect in his wife which permits annulment. He has to be satisfied with the option to divorce her if he lost hope in curing her, because the life of the couple is based on the mutual right to enjoyment, and this is not denied when the wife is inflicted with mental disease or epilepsy. Likewise, the husband has no right to charge the wife or her guardian with anything, when she becomes handicapped.

In sum: the son of the asker in this case has no charge against his wife or any of her guardians because she became sick. All he has to do is either endure her companionship with patience, or separate from her via divorce. In the last option, she deserves all the Sharʿī rights of a divorcee. And God may He be praised and exalted knows best.

X. The Siwāk

Al-Iʿtiṣām
December 1985-January 1986, pp. 30-31
by ʿAbd Al-Tawwāb Yūsuf

> The latest European invention in tooth-pastes. After several centuries Switzerland discovers the big secret behind the *miswāk* which purifies the mouth and kills pathogens.

Days and months, years and centuries pass, and the words of Muḥammad b. ʿAbd Allah are confirmed to be true. The modern science proves the rightfulness of what he has said and the perfection of his sayings, since he was inspired by Allah and spoke of all that is astonishing and eternal.

This was the thought that entered my mind when I examined a box of toothpaste imported from Switzerland...You may be smiling and amazed about the connection between all this and my thoughts ... what was written on the box answers best the amazement.

> A tooth-paste which includes the extract of *miswāk* clean of any splinters and which has been scientifically proven to be effective in killing harmful mouth pathogens...

I stopped at the word *miswāk* ... which I did no longer read or see ... it disappeared from our modern life as a result of the spread of the toothbrush. They teach us that it is called *farjūn*. The paste which tens of advertisements teach us of its various types—is, according to the ads, the only one which contains certain ingredients. They resort to a picture of a pretty girl with red lips and white teeth, which look like pearls inside her smiling mouth, in order to convince us of the magic work of this tooth-paste.

The *miswāk*! Thank you Switzerland! you reminded me of it ... Moreover, there is a picture of it on the box, the bark was removed from one edge and it is ready for use exactly as I used to see my father use it. The same words appear on the box in English and French as well. Allah knows how moved I was when I saw the word "*miswāk*" printed in three languages: Arabic, English, French. The attached brochure in the three languages is headed by the Prophetic hadith: "*Siwāk* is a purifier for the mouth and a source of satisfaction for the Lord."

The brochure says:

> This is one of many noble prophetic traditions, in which the Prophet Muḥammad recommended to use the *siwāk* for cleaning the teeth.

In the research department of the Swiss company for pharmaceutics located in Basle, Switzerland, under the supervision of scientists, among whom is a Muslim Arab specialist doctor (I was told by private sources that he is Egyptian), the scientific experiments on the extract of *miswāk* were conducted. The results were surprising yet decisive that the *miswāk*, scientifically termed "sulfa duraberzika" contains chemicals which kill the harmful bacteria in the mouth, which causes gingival inflammation, pathogens and caries.

The brochure continues:

> The research department at the Swiss Company isolated some harmful splinters from the extract of the *miswāk* ... so that the "paste" fits all gums, including those of children. This became the first paste in the world containing the extract of pure natural *miswāk*. It does not include any dangerous chemicals, and it provides a clear scientific proof for the wisdom of Arabs and Islam...

The last comment at the end of the brochure says:

> The color of the paste which is yellowish is because of the extract of the natural *miswāk* which the paste contains, and it does not have any impact on the color of the teeth and not on its strong activity in whitening them...

Anyway we are not interested in advertising a new tooth-paste ... though we are delighted at every chance of furthering knowledge on matters related to Islamic and Arabic culture, consequently we approach Islamic companies and institutions to help us with the expenses of paper and the high costs of printing. We are here to promote something that we have longed for, and wished and hoped that our scientists ... we always tell them "make use of the Islamic and Arabic heritage ... We are certain that they preceded us after the distance between us and them had been huge ... huge ... but Western civilization has caught up with us, overtaken us and benefited from our contributions to human scientific heritage ... There is nothing wrong in it but what is wrong is that we have given up our heritage and that we do not cling to it with our fingers and that we do not hold on to it with our teeth. We have deserted it so that the West can embrace it and benefit from it, while we observe from the side, astonished ... and possibly we also compliment them out of foolishness.

This doctor or Egyptian pharmacist is an Arab and a Muslim, and is aware of the heritage ... he was inspired with it ... he absorbed it ... used it ... and we will never blame him or scold him ... for carrying what he "discovered" to Swiss factories. Probably he has encountered here difficulties, problems, and obstacles that pushed him to offer the invention to the famous Swiss companies and to factories which are free of administrative complications and which are not governed by bureaucracy and whose pharmacists and their unions do not struggle with the pharmaceutical companies in the quest for "private profit" ...and let the patients die! Their companies know what science is, and they opened their heart to this person who clung to the dignified tradition about the *miswāk* ... which millions [of people] have uttered over the years ... but only one person found in it something which humanity at large can enjoy ... Did Newton, Addison and other genius inventors do anything different than that?

The *miswāk* was a wonderful educational lesson when the Prophet held it and started "reproaching" his servant who was close to him, and could hear him when he called, but did not respond ... The Messenger of God said to her pointing to the *miswāk* that was in his hand: "Were I not afraid of *qiṣāṣ* (retaliation) I could have caused you pain with it!

Your mercy, Messenger of God ... can this little soft *miswāk* cause pain?

Shame on your great belief, oh Messenger of God. Are you afraid that God would retaliate if you punished a girl with *miswāk*? He knows well that those who help us in our deeds are part of us, and we are part of them ... no difference ... no discrimination ... we are all equal ... no one is better than the other, but in their belief and good deeds...

The *miswāk* had also a role in army and at war ... In one of the raids the *mushrikūn* (polytheists) noticed some Muslims clean their teeth by *miswāk*. This scared the *Mushrikūn* who thought that the Muslims were sharpening their teeth in order to prey on them. The *mushrikūn*'s power was reduced by that and this was one of the reasons for their defeat and for the Muslims' victory.

The *miswāk* was not useful only for medicine and healing ... it also contributed to education, psychology and it is a means for winning a military battle.

Your reward, Egyptian-Arab Muslim physician will come from Allah, for the proper exploitation of your knowledge and the knowledge of former Muslims headed by the trustworthy Messenger Muḥammad b. ʿAbd Allah.[41]

[41] A detailed study of the *siwāk* and its special qualities can be found in my "The *Siwāk*: A Medieval Islamic Contribution to Dental Care", in: *The Journal of the Royal Asiatic Society* (of Great Britain and Ireland), 3rd series, Vol. 2, Part 1, April 1992, pp. 13-20.

CHAPTER THIRTEEN

SUMMARY

Medicine is a universal science, intended everywhere to sustain or better human health. The level of medical treatment offered to its "consumers" anywhere is mainly a function of the available resources at a particular place and time.

Medical ethics, however, depends less on resources and more on the particular religious and philosophical trends. The medical ethics of Islam, as shown in the foregoing chapters, is colored by shades of Islamic dogma and Sharʿī law. Islamic medical ethics is not exceptional in its exclusiveness. One may also speak of Jewish, Catholic and Protestant medical ethics, as well as Buddhist and Hindu medical ethics.

Therefore, any religion, but especially religions which provide legal instructions concerning the daily conduct of the believer (such as Judaism and Islam), also intervene in the ethical approach expected of the believer when he/she faces medical dilemmas.

Islamic medical ethics is therefore necessarily linked to the Islamic religion. Consequently, one cannot fully comprehend Islamic ethics on abortion, organ transplant, autopsy and euthanasia, for example, without first understanding the Islamic philosophical-religious perception of the human body, the value of human life, and the meaning of death and of life after death as taught by the Qur'an, the Hadith and the legal literature.

Likewise, one cannot understand the Islamic ethical position on artificial insemination, doctor-patient relations, circumcision and AIDS, without first considering the Islamic attitude toward sex, male-female relations, the position of marriage in Islamic society and the stability which a strong and close family unit is believed to provide for society at large.

To a certain degree I admit, as Tristram Engelhardt Jr. claimed, that "Bioethics is an element of a secular culture and the great-grandchild of the Enlightenment" at least in its most recent appearance. But I cannot agree with his thesis that "bioethics, unlike many codes of ethics, tends not to be national or parochial, because these developments in health care and in the biomedical sciences are tied generally to the development of industrial societies... As it addresses this wide range of societies and their difficulties with 'Western' biomedicine, bioethics draws on a tradition of the West that in fact attempts to step outside the constraints of particular cultures, including Western culture itself, by giving reasons and arguments anyone should accept. In this sense, bioethics is a general attempt in secular ethics."[1]

Engelhardt may be right in that the general topics and questions which contemporary bioethics addresses seem to recur in various societies. He is not right with regard to the solutions and nuances which each ethical code finds for those questions. These, after all, are the ones that matter—those that influence practice.

There is no doubt that the modern media contribute to the introduction of the ethical dilemmas into remote areas, hence into various religious and other communities. The solutions, to be applicable, must nevertheless be locally and independently provided in each society or religious community. This does not prevent the occurrence of certain similarities among various ethical codes. But such similarities should not be understood as an attempt to satisfy one common universal code.

Moreover, even within what seems to be a single religious ethical code, such as the Islamic, we have found several trends which mirror philosophical, legal and political disagreements among members of the same religious community. This testifies that the ethical code is being constantly shaped and reshaped, that it never reaches a final stage, and that it needs always to be reassessed against a defined chronological or temporal framework in order to be considered valid. The study of any ethical code can never lead to absolute conclusions, but only to relative ones, pertaining to time and place.

Therefore, one finds ancient Greek medical ethics, Biblical ethics versus contemporary halakhic ethics, and contemporary African or Western ethics, with an emphasis on the relevant period of applicability.

Within Islamic medical ethics we can speak of "popular ethics," a product of lay people, versus "legally authorized ethics," a product of scholars, jurists, doctors and scientists. One may debate over which of

---

[1] H. Tristram Engelhardt Jr., "The emergence of a secular bioethics", in: Tom L. Beauchamp and Le Roy Walters (eds.), *Contemporary Issues in Bioethics*, 3rd edition, USA 1988, pp. 65-67.

the two types came first to the world and which has attracted more followers...

From "popular ethics" we learn, for example, that a complicated labor may be eased if the mother drinks water in which verses of the Qur'an and some vague phrases written earlier on china and ivory plates have been immersed. The religious scholars naturally view this as an imposture and a resort to magic.[2]

Another example of "popular ethics" is the belief that if sick people offer a supplication to God in certain locations in Egypt, they are immediately cured. This, again, is refuted by the jurists, on the grounds that it contradicts the locations which God himself has selected for responding to the believers' supplications.[3] "Scientific" or "semi-scientific" medical ethics is the type authorized by scholars and jurists as legitimate.

The Islamic code of chastity, for example, represented by the *ḥijāb* (head-cover), is defended "scientifically" by the claim that it protects women's hair from damage, falling out and the ravages of weather.[4] In other words, the ethical code of chastity is shown to be in agreement with the latest scientific advances, hence doubly valid.

The prohibition of eating pork is explained "scientifically" as a medical measure against the intestinal disease cysticercosis, which afflicts pork-eaters only and whose symptoms are weakening of heart muscle, eye muscle or the brain, leading to a slowing of the heartbeat and blood circulation, loss of vision, paralysis or epilepsy.

Another disease caused by eating pork is trichinosis, the symptoms of which are vomiting, diarrhea, muscle pains, high fever, swelling of the skin, difficulty in breathing and even death in complicated cases of pneumonia and decelerated heartbeat.[5] The dietary laws of Islam are given reinforcement through the "scientifically"-based ethics, just as the chastity laws were validated earlier.

While the "scientific" or "juristic" type of ethics is relatively easy to follow because it is often expressed in writings, the exposition of "popular" ethics is usually a task for anthropologists. Only when the "scientific/juristic" type disagrees with the "popular" code of medical ethics can we learn about the latter from written sources as well, or

---

[2] *Majallat Al-Tawḥīd*, Jumādā Al-Ākhira 1411, p. 19 (the *muftī* is Muḥammad 'Alī 'Abd Al-Raḥīm).

[3] *Majallat Al-Tawḥīd*, Shawāl 1411, p. 18 (the same *muftī* as above).

[4] *Al-Ahrām*, January 19, 1990 (based on a new study).

[5] *Risālat Al-Islām*, March 1986, pp. 49-50 (Dr. Maḥmūd Aḥmad Najīb).

when a lay person innocently asks the *muftī* about something "popular" which the asker is not aware of its "popularity", and the *muftī* points to it.

The average person hardly gives himself/herself an account of whether certain ethics are "popular" or scientifically approved or grounded in the *Sharīʿa*.

More educated people may sometimes realize that certain ethics are not *Sharīʿ*-based and might therefore be of "popular" origins, but even they would expect the *muftī* so to state and to make this classification clear. The *muftī*s usually laud the scientific and *Sharʿi* proven ethics in an attempt to appear reasonable, enlightened and progressive themselves, and to enforce the *Sharīʿa* in lieu of the primitive superstitions which are often labeled as *bidʿa*.

There are however, complex cases, such as the belief in talismans and in the healing powers of certain prayers and nutritive elements, which have proofs in the Prophetic medicine and therefore cannot be easily dismissed. These do not allow a clear cut classification of "popular"/bad from "proven"/ good ethics. This is when the *muftī* himself is ambivalent, and each individual has then to make his/her own choices.

As already suggested, the best source for the contemporary code of medical ethics is the *fatāwā* literature in its various forms (individual *muftī* collections, annual *fatāwā* collections, sporadic *fatāwā*, special religious columns in periodicals and newspapers, etc.). This is because the *fatwā* is relatively a short compilation, easy to distribute, and so easy to recite or refute. Since the *fatwā* is a recommendation only, sometimes contradictory recommendations can co-exist, and the reader indirectly receives a wider picture of the religious-cultural situation.

The *fatwā,* even in response to what seems on the surface to be the concern of one individual, opens a window to the culture and mentality of Muslims as a group. *Fatāwā* are made public either in writings or in broadcasting, while the identity of the asker may be concealed upon necessity or request for privacy. The published *fatāwā* are accessible to all, especially to the literates and to the jurists, and the *fatwā* establishes a legal precedent.

The literary genre of the *fatāwā* is regenerative and never reaches an end. That is because each *fatwā* may become a basis for further debate or for further approval which are expressed in new *fatāwā*.

Each individual *fatwā* should be treated as a "single pearl" in the sense that it is an independently valuable piece and can teach us a lot, even when it is short, succinct and has no counterparts for the sake of comparison.

The researcher though should always expect that no *fatwā* is the only one on a topic, although another *fatwā* on the subject may not have been found yet.

It would therefore be a pretense on behalf of any researcher, including myself, to believe that either all the *fatāwā* of one *muftī*, or of one period or of one geographic location have been assembled by him/her.

Rather, whatever is available, in content and quantity, should be studied well for its social, economic, political and other imports—whether overt or implied.

From the case of a woman permitted to pay for her husband's medical treatment from her personal capital, we learn indirectly that women's private property is still sanctioned by law and society today, and that the husband is not entitled to benefit from it under any circumstances unless his wife generously concurs.[6]

Questions concerning fertility such as "What should I do if my fifth born child is a girl too and my husband threatens to divorce me?"[7] or "My daughter married a man who was found after marriage to be incapable of sexual intercourse: what should be legally done?"[8] can teach us something of the status of women, of expectations from sex, and of male-female relations in contemporary Islamic society.

Regardless of the form in which the *fatwā* was made public, all medical *fatāwā* seem to demonstrate a pragmatic approach. The most frequent principle employed by the *muftīs* is *al-ḍarūrāt tubīḥ al-maḥẓūrāt* ("necessities render the prohibited permitted"). This principle allows flexibility in practice, when the law seems strict and might lead to conservatism. In fact, this principle reaffirms the medieval legal principles of *maṣlaḥa* (public interest), namely, provided that the public benefits and no major Islamic principle is violated, a new idea or method may be admitted into the code of proper Islamic conduct. By this principle Islamic medical ethics has legitimized artificial insemi-

---

[6] *Al-Jumhūriyya*, January 31, 1991, p. 14 (Dr. 'Abd Al-Mawjūd 'Abd Al-Laṭīf).

[7] *Al-Muslimūn*, July 12, 1991, p. 8.

[8] *Al-Nūr*, September 27, 1989, p. 8 (*muftī* 'Abd Allah Al-Mushidd).

nation, organ transplants, postmortems and the use of certain medications and advanced medical treatments.

The Islamic code of medical ethics has been formulated with great sensitivity to human nature and needs. It has also demonstrated a good acquaintance with the achievements of Western medicine in general and with the code of Western medical ethics: both are often recognized as the highest degree of human scientific progress and thinking, respectively, although for reasons grounded in Islamic law and theology they are not always feasible for Muslims.

The study of medical ethics nowadays cannot be separated from the study of human rights. Privacy, personal dignity, making one's own choices, living freely, dying peacefully; ownership, childbearing, seeking medical help and hence improving the quality of one's life—these are only a few of the rights intimated in the previous chapters.

The Western code of medical ethics, influenced by Western law, rationalism and history, and perhaps by what Max Weber already in 1904 termed "the Protestant Ethic," emphasizes the rights of the individual more than the Islamic code. Therefore, euthanasia and surrogate motherhood, the most extreme examples, may win some legitimacy in the West, but none under the Islamic code of ethics.

But it would be unfair to conclude that Islamic medical ethics ignores human rights altogether. We have seen that special care is given to individual cases of women who must abort their fetuses because of pressing reasons, although an abortion is never a desired method. We also found that plastic surgeries intended to solve emotional and psychological problems, are legitimized despite the theological encouragement not to change the form of the body as created. Postmortems are legitimized to fulfil the right to justice or to obtain additional scientific knowledge, despite the Sharʿī prescription of speedy burial and preservation of the body unmutilated. Most organ transplants are permitted to save life, if the donor's own right to live is not thereby believed violated. Many more examples can be supplied in support of the attention shown in Islamic medical ethics to the individual human condition.

It is also true, however, that Islamic medical ethics, unlike the Western code of medical ethics, often identifies the rights of the individual with those of society at large. In other words, protection of the individual's human right entails protection of the right of society as a whole: if the wife is circumcised her husband's right to her loyalty is guaranteed, and at the same time the structure of society as a whole is rewarded through the prevention of *zinā*, which female circumcision is believed to promote.

An autopsy, when legitimized, can indeed solve the mystery of an individual's sudden death. But unless justice as a supreme value in Islamic society is done, and unless medical students benefit from the knowledge acquired by that particular dissection and later on utilize it for the welfare of society, the autopsy would not have been legitimized.

An abortion for the sake of better planning the family is sometimes justified in order "to produce fewer but more qualitative offspring." But at other times such an abortion may be denied legitimacy because "it reduces the Islamic ranks." In both cases the interest of society is mentioned parallel to the consideration of the individual's situation.

An exception to the above generalization is produced by the discussion of AIDS. Here, no sympathy is given to the rights of those already afflicted by the disease. The consideration is solely to protect the rights of society, which is still unafflicted but threatened by the misconduct or perversion of those stricken. The AIDS disease has definitely been found by Muslim jurists to be a useful tool to accuse Western civilization of failing to educate its members, and by contrast to laud the Islamic success in educating Muslims.

The Islamic approach to AIDS patients will be better understood if rather than being treated as a purely medical issue, AIDS is studied as a representative of Islamic ethical attitudes to those who dare break social taboos, and who by their acts endanger the sanctified solid structure of Islamic society.

Recently it has been suggested that just as God's punishment for perverts is AIDS, God's punishment for wine drinkers is sudden blindness. This handily explained twelve cases of sudden blindness among wine drinkers in Cairo. The bottom line of the *fatwā* which reported this observation was that all sales of wine must be outlawed.[9]

The last *fatwā* demonstrates the apologetic and reproaching roles which are so often linked to today's *fatāwā*, and especially to those of medical import. It also underlines the futility of any attempt to disconnect the medical ethics formulated by Muslims and for Muslims from the tenets of their religion and legal system.

---

[9] *Al-Ḥaqīqa*, July 27, 1991, p. 7.

APPENDIX: NEWSPAPERS AND PERIODICALS

Al-Ahrām (Egypt). Founded in 1876 and a daily newspaper since 1881, representing a wide range of opinions.

Al-Daʿwa (Egypt). A publication of the Muslim Brotherhood.

Al-Daʿwa (Saudi Arabia). A weekly founded in 1965, specializing in Islamic religion.

Al-Ḥaqīqa (Egypt). A weekly.

Hudā Al-Islām (Jerusalem). Islamic-Educational bimonthly.

Al-Islām waṭan (Egypt). A monthly, published by the ʿAzmī Sufi order.

Al-Iʿtiṣām (Egypt). An Islamic monthly.

Al-Jumʿa (Egypt). Published by *Al-Jamʿiyya Al-Sharʿiyya liTaʿāwun al-ʿĀmilīn bil-Kitāb wal-Sunna al-Muḥammadiyya* (The religious association of the followers of Qur'an and Sunna).

Al-Jumhūriyya (Egypt). A daily newspaper since 1953. Since 1970 it has followed a leftist orientation.

Liwāʾ Al-Islām (Egypt). A monthly for more than 45 years.

Al-Liwāʾ Al-Islāmī (Egypt). A weekly, since 1981 attached to the daily newspaper *Māyū* to speak against fundamentalist circles.

Majallat Al-Azhar (Egypt). A monthly published by the Islamic Research Center at Al-Azhar.

Majallat Al-Tawḥīd (Egypt). A monthly Islamic cultural publication of the *Jamāʿat Anṣār Al-Sunna Al-Muḥammadiyya* (Supporters of the Sunna).

Manār Al-Islām (Abu Dhabi, U.A.E.). A monthly published by the Ministry of Islamic Affairs (*Wizārat Al-Shuʾūn Al-Islāmiyya wAl-Awqāf*).

Māyū (Egypt). A daily since 1981; a publication of *Al-Ḥizb Al-Waṭanī Al-Dīmuqrāṭī* (The National Democratic Party).

Minbar Al-Islām (Egypt). A monthly, published by the Ministry of Awqāf.

Al-Mukhtār Al-Islāmī (Egypt). A monthly founded in 1979.

Al-Muslimūn (Saudi Arabia). International Muslims' weekly.

Al-Nūr (Egypt). A weekly since 1982, published by the Liberal party (*Al-Aḥrār*).

Al-Taṣawwuf Al-Islāmī (Egypt). An Islamic monthly, published by the Supreme Sufi Council (*Al-Majlis Al-Ṣūfī Al-Aʿlā*).

Al-Umma (Egypt). A biweekly since 1984, published by *Al-Umma* party.

Al-Umma Al-Islāmiyya (Egypt). A monthly since 1982, attached to *Al-Akhbār*.

INDEX OF *MUFTĪS*' NAMES

Social, Economic and Political Studies of the Middle East/Études sociales, économiques et politiques du Moyen-Orient

This series includes studies, collaborative volumes and reference works, by social scientists of diverse disciplines as well as historians, concerning the culture and societies, economies and polities of the Middle East today. The past is covered insofar as leading up to the present. Volumes in the series deal preferentially with topics and issues of interest to both the scholarly community and the public. Case studies and specialist works are included occasionally.

EDITED BY C.A.O. VAN NIEUWENHUIJZE

1. NIEUWENHUIJZE, C.A.O. VAN. *Sociology of the Middle East.* A stocktaking and interpretation. 1971. ISBN 90 04 02564 2
2. ZUWIYYA, J. *The parliamentary election of Lebanon* 1968. 1972. ISBN 90 04 03460 9
3. MANSUR, F. *Bodrum, a town in the Aegean.* 1972. ISBN 90 04 03424 2
4. CHARNAY, J.-P. *Islamic culture and socio-economic change.* 2nd impr. 1981. ISBN 90 04 06488 5
5. FRY, M.J. *Finance and development planning in Turkey.* 1972. ISBN 90 04 03462 5
6. KHALAF, S. and P. KONGSTAD. *Hamra of Beirut.* A case of rapid urbanization. 1973. ISBN 90 04 03548 6
7. KARPAT, K.H. (ed.). *Social change and politics in Turkey.* A structural-historical analysis. 1973. ISBN 90 04 03817 5
8. WEIKER, W.F. *Political tutelage and democracy in Turkey.* The Free Party and its aftermath. 1973. ISBN 90 04 03818 3
9. BENEDICT, P., E. TÜMERTEKIN and F. MANSUR (eds.). *Turkey.* Geographic and social perspectives. 1974. ISBN 90 04 03889 2
10. ENTELIS, J.P. *Pluralism and party transformation in Lebanon*: Al-Kata'ib, 1936-1970. 1974. ISBN 90 04 03911 2
11. KARPAT, K.H. (ed.). *The Ottoman state and its place in world history.* 1974. ISBN 90 04 03945 7
12. BENEDICT, P. *Ula, an Anatolian town.* 1974. ISBN 90 04 03882 5
13. AMIN, G.A. *The modernization of poverty.* A study in the political economy of growth in nine Arab countries, 1945-1970. Photomech. repr. 1980. ISBN 90 04 06193 2
14. LANDAU, J.M. *Radical politics in modern Turkey.* 1974. ISBN 90 04 04016 1
15. FRY, M.J. *The Afghan economy.* Money, finance, and the critical constraints to economic development. 1974. ISBN 90 04 03986 4

16. KRANE, R.E. (ed.). *Manpower mobility across cultural boundaries.* Social, economic and legal aspects. The case of Turkey and West Germany. 1975. ISBN 90 04 04008 0
17. KARPAT, K.H. (ed.). *Turkey's foreign policy in transition, 1950-1974.* 1975. ISBN 90 04 04323 3
19. ABADAN-UNAT, N. (ed.). *Turkish workers in Europe, 1960-1975.* A socio-economic reappraisal. 1976. ISBN 90 04 04478 7
20. STAFFA, S.J. *Conquest and fusion.* The social evolution of Cairo A.D. 642-1850. 1977. ISBN 90 04 04774 3
21. NIEUWENHUIJZE, C.A.O. VAN (ed.). *Commoners, climbers and notables.* A sampler of studies on social ranking in the Middle East. 1977. ISBN 90 04 05065 5
22. GREEN, A.H. *The Tunisian ulama 1873-1915.* Social structure and response to ideological currents. 1978. ISBN 90 04 05687 4
23. STARR, J. *Dispute and settlement in rural Turkey.* An ethnography of law. 1978. ISBN 90 04 05661 0
24. El-MESSIRI, S. *Ibn al-Balad.* A concept of Egyptian identity. 1978. ISBN 90 04 05664 5
25. ISRAELI, R. *The public diary of President Sadat.* 3 parts.
    1. The road to war. 1978. ISBN 90 04 05702 1
    2. The road of diplomacy: the continuation of war by other means. 1978. ISBN 90 04 05865 6
    3. The road of pragmatism. 1979. ISBN 90 04 05866 4
26. EISENMAN, R.H. *Islamic law in Palestine and Israel.* A history of the survival of Tanzimat and Sharīᶜa in the British Mandate and the Jewish State. 1978. ISBN 90 04 05730 7
28. ALLMAN, J. *Social mobility, education and development in Tunisia.* 1979. ISBN 90 04 05875 3
29. GRANDIN, N. *Le Soudan nilotique et l'administration britannique.* Éléments d'interprétation socio-historique d'une expérience coloniale. 1982. ISBN 90 04 06404 4
30. ABADAN-UNAT, N., D. KANDIYOTI and M.B. KIRAY (ed.). *Women in Turkish society.* 1981. ISBN 90 04 06346 2
31. LAYISH, A. *Marriage, divorce and succession in the Druze family.* A study based on decisions of Druze arbitrators and religious courts in Israel and the Golan Heights. 1982. ISBN 90 04 06412 5
32. TOPRAK, B. *Islam and political development in Turkey.* 1981. ISBN 90 04 06471 0
33. El-MEHAIRY, T. *Medical doctors.* A study of role concept and job satisfaction. The Egyptian case. 1984. ISBN 90 04 07038 9
34. ATIŞ, S.M. *Semantic structuring in the modern Turkish short story.* An analysis of *The Dreams of Abdullah Efendi* and other short stories by Ahmet Hamdi Tanpinar. 1983. ISBN 90 04 07117 2
35. PARLA, T. *The social and political thought of Ziya Gökalp, 1876-1924.* 1985. ISBN 90 04 07229 2
36. KAMALI, M.H. *Law in Afghanistan.* A study of the constitutions, matrimonial law and the judiciary. 1985. ISBN 90 04 07128 8

37. NIEUWENHUIJZE, C.A.O. VAN. *The lifestyles of Islam.* Recourse to classicism—need of realism. 1985. ISBN 90 04 07420 1
38. FATHI, A. (ed.). *Women and the family in Iran.* 1985. ISBN 90 04 07426 0
39. YOUSSEF, M. *Revolt against modernity.* Muslim zealots and the West. 1985. ISBN 90 04 07559 3
40. NIEUWENHUIJZE, C.A.O. VAN, M.F. AL-KHATIB, A. AZER. *The poor man's model of development.* Development potential at low levels of living in Egypt. 1985. ISBN 90 04 07696 4
41. SCHULZE, R. *Islamischer Internationalismus im 20. Jahrhundert.* Untersuchungen zur Geschichte der islamischen Weltliga. 1990. ISBN 90 04 08286 7
42. CHILDS, T.W. *Italo-Turkish diplomacy and the war over Libya, 1911-1912.* 1990. ISBN 90 04 09025 8
44. ZÜRCHER, E.J. *Political opposition in the early Turkish Republic.* The progressive Republican Party, 1924-1925. 1991. ISBN 90 04 09341 9
45. LIPOVSKY, I.P. *The Socialist Movement in Turkey 1960-1980.* 1992. ISBN 90 04 09582 9
46. RISPLER-CHAIM, V. *Islamic medical ethics in the twentieth century.* 1993. ISBN 90 04 09608 6